SAVOR EACH STITCH

Studio Quilting with Mindful Design

CAROLYN FRIEDLANDER

Published in 2014 by Lucky Spool Media, LLC

www.luckyspool.com
info@luckyspool.com

Published 2014 by Lucky Spool Media, LLC
P.O. Box 270142, Louisville, CO 80027
www.luckyspool.com
info@luckyspool.com

TEXT © Carolyn Friedlander
EDITOR Susanne Woods
ILLUSTRATIONS Carolyn Friedlander and Kari Vojtechovsky
PHOTOGRAPHY © Alexis Wharem, Greenprint Photography
DESIGNER Rae Ann Spitzenberger

9 8 7 6 5 4 3 2 1

First Edition
Printed and bound in the USA

Library of Congress Cataloging-in-Publication
Data available upon request

ISBN: 978-1-940655-01-7

CONTENTS

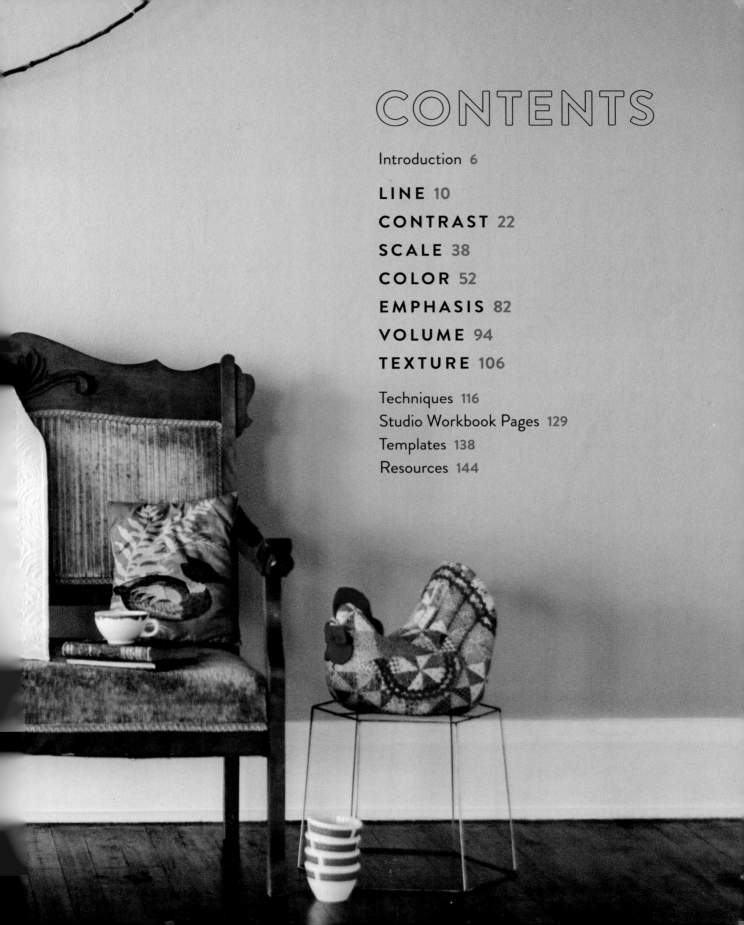

DEDICATION

It's really hard to believe that I am here writing this book. For a quiet, small-town girl, I never could have imagined being in a position wherein which I could teach and inspire others through my work. The fact that I *am* here and writing to you is the best example that I can give you of what can happen if you really believe in something. Sincerest thanks to everyone who has believed in me and supported my work. To my family and friends: your love and understanding is truly the backbone of any success that I may achieve. This book is dedicated to you.

I am grateful for the quilters who have come before us, and for all the quilters who will continue making quilts after us. We are all part of an amazing craft that is not only practical, but also a powerful means of expressing ourselves and the worlds we come from. My one wish is that we may each leave a mark that is uniquely our own.

ACKNOWLEDGMENTS

It's true that no great things get accomplished alone, and this book is a true testament of that. Sincerest thanks and much love to my family. To my parents, Edwin and Kathy, my Grandmother, Allen, Laurie, Keith, Cara, Jacob, and Samuel, your support means much more to me than you know. I am so lucky. To my friends—quilty and otherwise—I appreciate you all being crucial and supportive voices along this road with me. To Susanne, thank you for believing in me. I am grateful for you and the amazingly talented team that you've assembled at Lucky Spool. Thank you all for supporting my vision and for your part in this journey. I am happy and proud to be a part of your new journey as well. To Lexi of Greenprint Photography—we did it, and it was such a pleasure for me to get this chance to work with you! I consider it is a rare treat to find someone who you can trust and respect creatively the way I feel when working with you. I'm also so proud that us girls from Lake Wales have had this chance to show people our small place in the world. To the wonderful folks at Robert Kaufman, you guys continue to be such a joy to work with. Thank you for all the support and amazing fabrics to work with!

MY JOURNEY

FINDING YOUR PASSION

To be completely honest, I do not think it matters what you decide to do. What's more important is that you do something with passion and intention.

Quilt making does that for me, and I realized it during my first time sitting down at the sewing machine. I was absolutely addicted. A lot of things sucked me in—the beautiful fabrics, the feeling of actually working with my hands, the break from sitting at a computer and looking at a screen, the idea that I was drawing with thread and fabric, and knowing that I was doing something people have been doing for hundreds of years. It is an art, and knowing absolutely nothing means that there is so much to learn. To me, the very beginning of something is special. It is a new page, and you have so much to look forward to, learning and tackling as you move along. Quilt making was especially intriguing to me because it provides an abundance of tools to use and the flexibility to use them in a way to express myself.

Quilt making filled a void I was feeling in my daily life by satisfying my creative impulse and enthusiasm for working with my hands. It was the perfect creative outlet that I was looking for.

Growing up on a cattle and citrus ranch in central Florida, we had no neighbors and no TV, but what my brother, sister, and I did have was a 640-acre back yard and creative parents. I can actually remember a time as a kid that I complained to my mom about being bored. That was a terrible feeling.

It is funny to look back and think about that now, because it might have been the last time that I was actually really bored. It is also striking to reflect back and realize that my parents were never bored. They were both very active in their work and interests then, and they still are today.

Because of who they are, I know that my childhood complaint must have been instantly satisfied by something they had up their sleeves.

From my dad, I have learned about the satisfaction you can get from the work that you do. It also doesn't hurt to feel compelled and motivated by that work. He taught me the value of hard work. It's from him and my grandfather that I've inherited an entrepreneurial spirit that has inspired me to make a change in my career and build something that I really believe in.

Through my mom and the incredibly crafty women on her side of the family, I've had the most amazing exposure to sewing and to all kinds of making. My mom started sewing doll clothes as a child, and continued to sew her own clothes into adulthood. When we were kids, she made all of our clothes. It's been within the last couple decades that she has become a quilter. I have her to thank for my early exposure to both the sewing machine and fabric store--I have vivid memories of picking fabrics out with her for clothes. I was very young when I learned that the picture on the front of the pattern was not an absolute, but more like a suggestion. What a valuable lesson and example of putting your imagination to work by filling in your own blanks and making it your own.

As I began contemplating my own career path, I knew that I needed to do something creative, but I also wanted it to be based in academia too. Architecture seemed like an ideal fit in both of those regards. I loved the idea of finding an analytical and creative balance.

Studying architecture and art in college only stoked the flames of my creativity. In the architecture curriculum, the design studio is what roots as well as drives everything else. Studio was not only the physical space where you spent your time, but it was also the system from which you built your skills. Physically, you had a desk and small pin-up space, but more than that was the idea that you were on a creative journey to problem solve in ways that worked for you. The space and resources were there. You had to figure out how it made sense for you to use them. Looking back on that time in my life now, I realize that it was in studio where I found my voice as a designer. In studio we were given a set of tools, and allowed the freedom to work with them in our own way. And we practiced these things a lot. In doing that, I found my own process for expressing who I am in my work. It was not easy, but I learned that expressing yourself in any medium is all about practice.

When I was about to graduate, I was definitely scared to be done with school, not because I wanted it to last forever, but mostly because I feared that in practice it would be a struggle to have the same kind of creative freedom that I had in school. I knew that I would probably not be sitting around in the office, at my drafting board, contemplating each pass of charcoal for a rendering I would be putting together for my client. I knew that life in school granted me more creative

luxury than I would be able to find at any architecture firm.

Once I began my career in architecture, the part about my job that I enjoyed the most was connecting with clients to understand their needs better. Good design is all about problem solving creatively, and I liked figuring out the details in that equation for my clients. Unfortunately, a much larger portion of my job was handling other things that did not seem to satisfy my creative needs as much. Plus computer-based architecture lacked a couple big areas of interest for me—color and working with my hands. I have always wondered if I would like practicing architecture more if it were still being drawn by hand. Sitting behind a computer screen is no comparison to sitting behind a big drafting board with a pencil in hand. Where's the creative romance in that?

But then I found quilt making.

Finally, a place where I could feel my design limbs again like I did while I was in architecture school. Quilting encompassed everything that I loved about architecture, but with more. It was an instant connection, which ignited the passion to create and express myself again.

There is so much to making a quilt. Our quilts are stories about who we are, what is going on in our lives, and what matters most to us. I love everything about quilt making— the process, the colors, the textures, the history, the ways it brings us together. I love that every quilt maker is different, and our quilts reflect that.

QUILT MAKING AS A CAREER

In my new career as a designer of patterns and fabrics, I am often in the thick of preparing new designs—a routine that after working in the industry for a few seasons is starting to get more familiar, but certainly not any more comfortable. With the fast-paced deadlines, I often ask myself if this is really what I want to be doing.

It totally is.

I should preface that thought by admitting that life as a Quilter-In-My-Free-Time is a different beast than the quilter I have become, which is more the Will-Quilt-For-Food, or something like that. I am careful about pursuing a business grown from my passion. I work hard to support myself doing something that I care very much about, and so it is important for me to know why I choose to do what I do.

I have always found myself to be most appreciative and excited when I am in

situations where I want to push myself further. It is in those situations that I become curious to figure out solutions and therefore become totally engaged.

Quilt making provides it all for me. It is a practical activity—but also, the process of "making" is a place where I can ask all kinds of questions not only about construction, but also about aesthetics and representation. In doing so and in working with all of the components at play, I find out so much about myself and the quilters who have come before me.

Quilts rock.

USING THIS BOOK

I am intrigued by the impact of each layer in the quilt making process—both literally and figuratively. Quilt making is an art with an incredible amount of flexibility. Because of this, we can each make quilts that represent who we are and in our own way. And I think that is incredibly amazing.

Here, I build off that idea of each layer and focus on how each of our design choices within each layer affects the outcome. I have explored a series of projects that highlight the impact of each of these decisions by showing the same designs, each pushed in totally different directions. I want to encourage you to start thinking about ways to do that yourself with any pattern you encounter. I want to highlight some of the ways I break down a design so that you can do the same.

As I worked on the designs for this book, I got excited thinking about how much further you will push them in your own way. Your interpretation will be something I never would have thought of. Don't be scared to take a risk and try something that you are curious about (I remind myself to do this all the time).

Our tools—line, contrast, scale, emphasis, color, volume, and texture.

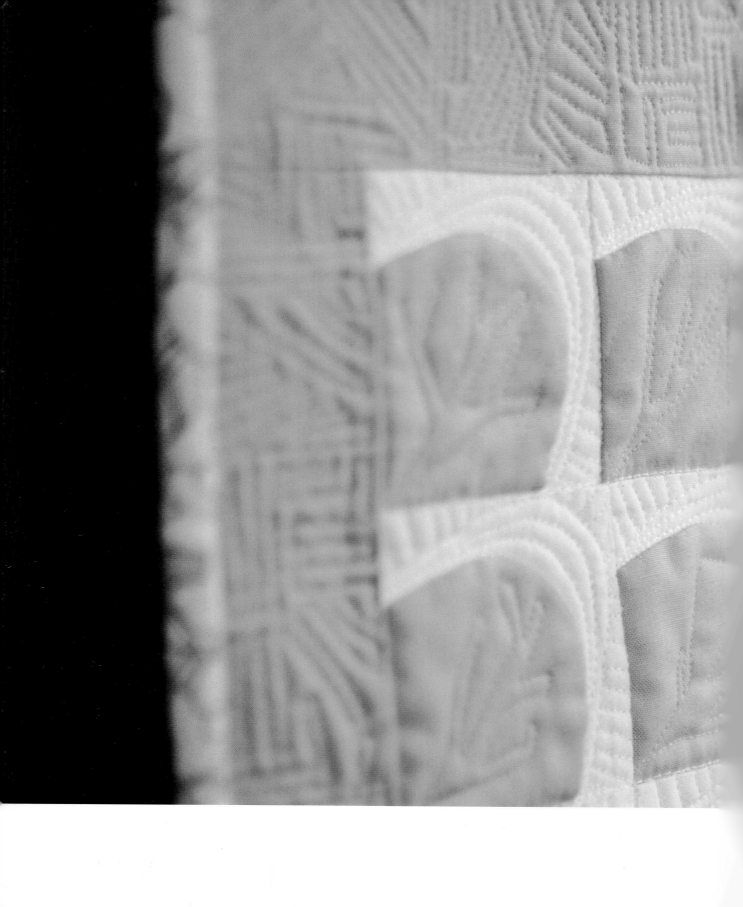

LINE

ALL DESIGNS START OUT AS A CENTRAL IDEA.

That idea can come from almost anywhere. It might be something that you have seen in nature, in your imagination, in the grocery store… wherever. Inspiration is everywhere.

The next step is to figure out how to represent that idea. When I am designing my quilts, I usually make use of my good buddy, the line, first and get to drawing. A line can say so much and have a personality all of its own.

In reducing an idea down to a single line (or set of lines), editing is an important component. Sometimes you have to be pretty ruthless. You want to be able to get to the point of your story and capture its essence without too many distractions.

One way that I do this is by working quickly when I first have an idea, knowing that refinement can come later. I try to get a lot of ideas on paper without getting too attached to anything too quickly. A blank page is always a tough place to begin, so jumping in at full speed helps take that edge off. It will get your mind moving and your ideas flowing.

TIP: Keep a sketchbook or camera handy to quickly capture inspirational ideas.

I find it helpful to keep a sketchbook to capture the initial idea or inspiration. Having just one sketchbook is probably ideal, but since I tend to forget to always have that one with me wherever I am, so I keep several in a few different places to make sure I am covered. It can be very useful to have a record of your thoughts that you can come back to later. Then, when you are ready to expand on the idea further, you can refer to your sketchbook and start to work at a larger scale and in a more focused way.

When I have a design that I am ready to explore, I usually get out a roll of paper and draw it over and over again until I get to the point of it making sense. As you work, certain things start to stand out and, hopefully, through this process, you will see your design begin to reveal itself.

To recap—everything should fit and speak to your goals. Start drawing like crazy and then edit until the answer is right in front of you.

Next step, fabric and thread give the drawings and your ideas life.

LINES IN QUILTING

SURFACE LINES | fabric, substrate

Taken literally, we find lines on fabric as well as in the substrate itself.

Printed fabrics can have printed lines, and coarsely woven fabrics such as linen can have textural lines from their composition and construction.

FOUNDATION LINES | pieced composition

We build lines into our work in the way we put things together. Think about what the lines you create in your piecing say in your overall composition.

STRUCTURAL LINES | quilting composition

Structurally, quilting is what finishes our quilts, but the process of quilting is very much line work. In fact, I became interested in free-motion quilting because it looked like drawing with a sewing machine. As we quilt, we use those lines to create emphasis, volume, and texture in our projects.

We can choose to make these lines recede or stand out depending on how we use them. Will there be a lot of them or very few? Will you use a thread to coordinate with the fabric or a thread to contrast?

DRAWING WORKSHOP

If you are not familiar or comfortable with drawing, here are a few things for you to think about:

1. Your drawings do not have to be perfect. Mine definitely aren't. Chances are that no one will even see your drawings or sketches unless you show them. They can be your little secret.

2. Drawing is really just a way of practicing how you see and think about something. It is only paper, and you can always start over.

3. With practice you will get better. I promise! Like everything else, you cannot expect to be an expert at something new, but the more you practice the more you will improve. When I try something new and I am not good at it, I love thinking about how much room for improvement I have. There is nowhere to go but up.

4. Drawing is the way of visualizing ideas that works for me, but there are many other tools you can use. Maybe you have a keen eye for photography and therefore creating collages of images is a good way for you to process your ideas. Or maybe you are best at verbalizing your thoughts and would do well keeping a journal. There are no rules; just use what works best and speaks to you!

SURFACE
LINES

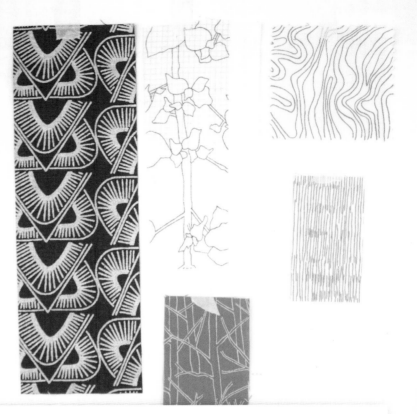

FOUNDATION
AND STRUCTURAL
LINES

PROJECT | In this project, you can manipulate lines in your fabric choices, piecing, and quilting, depending on what your goals might be. Maybe you love the lines created from the pieced shapes, and so you want to emphasize that in your own unique palette. Maybe you found some beautiful fabric that uses lines in a way that you think will perform well in the background of the blocks and border. Or maybe you are inspired by the design to explore line work in your quilting with some of your favorite thread. Raid your stash, go outside or head to your special place with your sketchbook. I am hopeful that this project will get your wheels turning! My original thought was for a basic clamshell shape, but as I started drawing lines to create the design, I discovered how the project could take on an entirely new personality by simply exaggerating the curve. I imagined how much those simple shapes could take on when adding color, print, and texture. Sometimes simple shapes can work really well in many different ways.

FLOWERS | big on small

The first version that I put together features a few large-scale floral prints in a close range of colors on a white textured background (it's actually the white crosshatch from my Architextures collection). The surface design on the printed fabric is not so much line based; rather, painted areas of color depict the flowers at a large scale. I love working with these types of prints because you can blend your pieced shapes into the background or into each other. Imagine how much more blended this version could be if I used a similar type print for the background. Everything would be softened even more.

WASABI | solids together

In the second version, I used a solid (Kona wasabi) on the same white textured background fabric that I used in the Flowers. Using a solid for the scale in this version enunciates that shape the most. It also gives you the most prominent platform to quilt as solids will showcase your quilted line work the most.

STRIPES | directions meet print

In the third version, I used stripes for the arcs and a Japanese print for the background that I cut into pieces and sewed back together in order. I am always curious to see how large-scale fabric prints will read when cut up and sewn. The motif in this one is relatively subtle, and the fact that I kept it together in the background reinforces that subtlety.

Stripes are as linear as you can get. I guess that's why I love working with them so much. Their directionality has implications that you can use to shape your project in some really fun ways. In this project, I chose striped fabrics in a variety of thicknesses and densities, and positioned them in the opposite direction of the length of the runner. If I arranged the stripes to run with the length of the runner, it would add to the length. Instead, I wanted the stripes to balance that flow rather than exaggerate it. The stripes are bold enough that using them this way slightly distorts the shape of the appliqué.

I also played with the direction of the stripes when I quilted the runner. In this case, the layer of quilting builds off of the fabric layer.

FLOWERS

WASABI

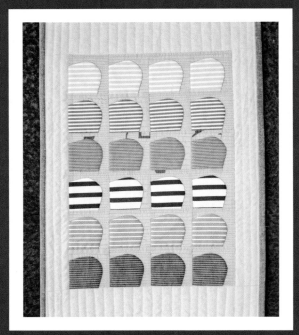

STRIPES

ARCS

Finished Block Size: 2½" x 2½"

Finished Quilt Size: 13½" x 22½"

MATERIALS

Background fabric: ¼ yard

Appliqué fabric(s): ¼ yard total

Border fabric: ¼ yard

Backing fabric: ¾ yard

Binding fabric: ¼ yard

Batting: 22" x 31"

PREPARATION

Copy full-size Arcs template (pullout page) onto template plastic, freezer paper, or cardstock, copying all notes onto template.

CUTTING INSTRUCTIONS

From background fabric, cut twenty-four 3" squares. From appliqué fabric(s), cut twenty-four 2½" squares with fabric(s) right side up. Align template on cut appliqué fabric square, matching straight edges. Mark curve and cut along the marked line. Cut arcs from all appliqué fabric squares.

If you want to use your fabric in a continuous way (like I did in the Stripes version), develop a system for noting the order of your fabrics as you cut them. Usually I use basic basting stitches and a variety of thread colors to denote row and block order (see below).

ASSEMBLE BLOCKS

Baste and sew arcs onto background squares using needle-turn appliqué (page 120).

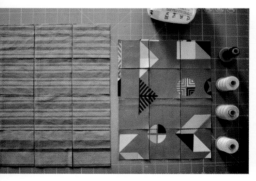

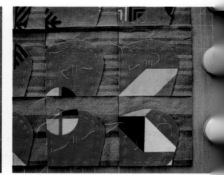

ASSEMBLE QUILT TOP

Lay out finished blocks as shown in Figure 1, with 4 columns across and 6 rows down. Sew blocks and rows together, pressing seams so they nest (page 119).

Refer to the Border Workshop (page 36) before attaching your borders.

Cut and attach 2" borders at long sides. Press seams toward borders. Cut and attach 4" borders at top and bottom. Press seams toward borders.

On the Stripes version, I pressed the borders toward the blocks to create a "fuller" inset. Using a lighter Japanese fabric as the background and a heavier border fabric made that very easy to do. Plus, it makes sense to push the seam allowances toward the less bulky fabric.

QUILT FINISHING

Baste and quilt as desired. Cut binding fabric into 2 strips 2½" wide and see page 128 for finishing instructions.

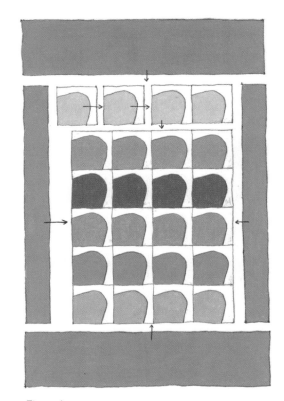

Figure 1

MACHINE APPLIQUÉ WORKSHOP

This book focuses on hand appliqué because that's what I love doing. If you're not a hand sewer, the same projects can be easily constructed using machine appliqué instead. Where the instructions indicate needle-turning the edges, use a machine satin stitch, blind stitch or other decorative stitch to finish the edges.

In addition, if you prefer to hold appliqué pieces in place using fusible web instead of hand basting or pinning, that works as well for machine-finished edges.

Quilters aren't all cut from the same cloth, so to speak, so there are always other methods to try and see what's most comfortable for you.

CONTRAST

CONTRAST IS A POWERFUL TOOL TO HAVE IN YOUR DESIGN TOOLBOX. It may sound like a simple concept, but it can often be the difference between a so-so execution and one with much more impact.

In the most general sense, contrast is the value difference (light to dark) between two or more things. By learning how to manage contrast, you can successfully blend fabrics together (by using values with low levels of contrast) or make them really stand out (by using values with high amounts of contrast).

The other factor to remember when considering contrast (and actually with all of our tools) is that it is all relative. What you decide to put where really depends on the neighbors and the neighborhood you are creating. You have control over the final outcome of your designs, and playing with the contrast within a composition has a tremendous impact.

You can do a value check with your phone or other digital camera. Just take a picture of your fabric combination and convert the image to black and white. Analyze your selected range and make adjustments as needed.

TIP: If you filter a fabric image to gray scale, the contrast becomes more obvious.

Consider the fabric combinations shown on these pages. The swatches (below) show a wide range in contrast from black to white. Conversely, the white quilt (top at right) makes use of a much more limited and subtle range.

When looking at each combination individually, you see the differences in contrast. When put them together, the more limited range of contrast is harder to differentiate. You can use value in many ways in your projects. More narrow, subtle groupings of fabrics can convey calmness in addition to restraint and control, whereas a quilt with wider ranges of contrast can be dramatically expressive; when used together, one might negate or lessen the impact of the other.

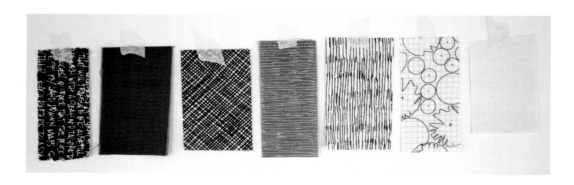

Two versions of Stripes (from my pattern
collection) show a wide range of contrast
with color as well as the impact a more
limited palette can make.

PROJECT | Simple, basic shapes are always a great place to start. For this design, I was thinking about appliquéd circles and how the top and bottom layers could work together to each tell a story. In order for each layer to convey its own part of the story, it would need to have a large enough area to make an impact. So I layered different sizes of circles with two fabrics, one for the appliqué and the other for the background. To make it more interesting and to create less of an emphasis on the circle itself, I split the circles into quadrants and positioned the inner arcs so they would not match up but still ensuring that the outer arcs match in order to define the circle. It has always been a challenge for me to find a use for 10-inch pre-cut squares, but this project became the perfect platform for using them. By using a 10-inch square for the appliqué, the blocks would be large enough to create some interesting variations.

BULLS-EYE

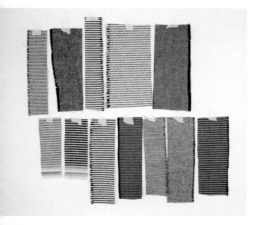

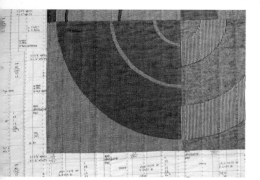

RAILROAD | equally striped

There is not a lot of contrast within the block fabrics in this version. They are all part of the same family, related in value and genre. However, the border is another story, and it appealed to me because of its departure from that value and genre.

While I worked on this design, I realized that the fabric was reminiscent of a deconstructed pair of jeans. Fabric can be very inspiring, and when I saw these Railroad denims, I was enticed by the textures and shades of indigo but they still hinted at that same utilitarian wonderfulness. Plus they are stripes. You may have guessed that I am often drawn to stripes. (Lines, anyone?)

When using stripes, they have the potential to get visually crazy. When you work with them, be aware of that and be careful to play it to your advantage. In this quilt, I made sure that all my stripes were going in the same direction. Stripes convey movement and direction, and I didn't want that to be distracting and cause any more movement than the design already had. My focus for this project was contrast, and since I wanted to explore some combinations that are more subtle, I needed to use my stripes as a uniting element instead of a competing force.

The borders in this project are generous. Space can offer breathing room, provide a barrier, allow for a transition, or create a frame. The more functional reason why I added wide borders to this project, was to create a decent-size quilt for curling up with on the couch. While auditioning fabrics for this version, I loved the way the gray ledger print spoke to the striped, utilitarian theme already going on. It freshened up the palette and made for an interesting contrast in scale and aesthetic.

I chose to hand quilt this version using the big-stitch method and perle cotton thread. I love that big-stitch introduces new colors in the thick threads. It is yet another layer that adds dimension and texture. Here, the copper threads are another throwback to that perfectly worn-in pair of jeans. The extra bit of warm color was just what this otherwise cool and neutral palette needed.

As I was quilting, the texture of the project became soft and worn—just like a pair of jeans. You can be surprised by how well your decisions play out in your projects. That is a testament to following your gut. If you are drawn to doing something a certain way, then go with it. The results might surprise you.

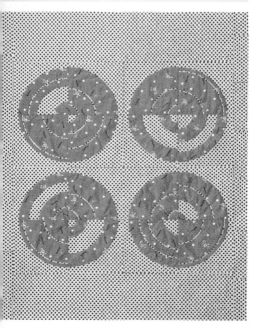

JAPANESE POLKA DOTS | print vs. print

This version has the highest level of contrast, even though both fabrics when used together might throw you for a loop. I used two bold prints, both of which have opposing figure and ground values. The polka-dot fabric has a light-value ground (cream), whereas the polka dots themselves have a dark, high value (red). The red fabric is the opposite. The figure—grid and flowers—is white, which is as low as you can go for value. The ground is that warm tangerine, which next to the white has a much darker value. When you squint your eyes you can see how the two fabrics' individual natures together create contrast. The polka-dot fabric reads lighter than the tangerine print.

Using the same two fabrics throughout diminishes any visual competition, providing the most distinct expression of the design itself. You will notice this especially if you take a look back at the Railroad version.

I decided to do something a little different with the borders. Instead of choosing a third fabric, I went back to the polka dots. This makes the bulls-eyes really pop out and float on a much larger, unrestricted plane. The quilting is intended to enhance this relationship. I did an allover motif in the background, working my way around each bulls-eye into all the nooks and crannies. The polka-dot background is somewhat busy, meaning that the dots move when you are looking at them. Quilting with any level of detail in this situation is less important because the dominance of the fabric disguises much of your stitching. It will also disguise your seams, making the background appear more united.

Tip: The threads you choose to quilt with can add another layer that plays with contrast. A thicker thread with a big-stitch will provide a different amount of physical and visual contrast than a machine stitch with smaller thread.

SCRAPPY | it's all game

I always love a scrappy project. When working with scraps, contrast is a very important consideration. You decide how much your design elements will stand out by either choosing fabrics close in value range to blend, or fabrics very different in value to stand out. In scrappy quilts, you can select more of a mix or you can play with both ideas and include every one of your favorite fabrics.

With this version, I made sure that each fabric played well with the others or spoke to the overall mood, while still making its own statement within each block. I achieved this by positioning a few fabrics block by block until I was happy with the result. I wasn't concerned that all the background was lighter than the appliqué. Instead, I made sure that each block worked on its own first and with the group second.

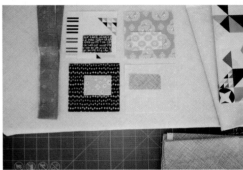

I looked at the borders as a frame. Sometimes when the fabrics and/or piecing are crazy on the inside, it is nice to unite the finished quilt with a decisive border. For this Scrappy version, I used a bold print from my Botanics collection that I hadn't used in any of the other blocks. The color related to the pieced fabrics, but I didn't have to worry about it blending into any of the blocks. I wanted the border to put an edge to the scrappiness and for the border to read as a flat frame. But maybe you do not want the border to blend into your bocks. In that case, I would recommend that you audition matching fabric from within the pieced design.

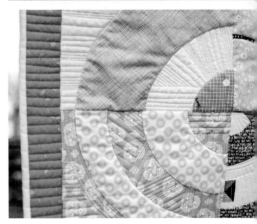

Tip: Have fun trying out a variety of swatches to start with before you narrow down your palette. As you narrow down your fabric selections, start thinking about each block and its placement.

BULLS-EYE

Finished Block Size: 10½" x 10½"

Finished Quilt Sizes: 54½" x 66½" throw, 25½" x 27" wall, 46½" x 49½" baby, 85½" x 93½" full/queen

Note: *Sizes are referred to in the following order: throw (wall, baby, full/queen).*

MATERIALS

Background fabric: 2 yards (¾ yard, 2 yards, 5 yards)

Appliqué fabric(s): 1¼ yards (⅜ yard, 1¼ yards, 3½ yards) total or 16 (4, 16, 48) pre-cut 10" squares

Border fabric: 1¾ yards (⅜ yard, ⅝ yard, 2¼ yards)

Backing fabric: 3½ yards (1 yard, 3⅛ yards, 8 yards)

Note: *For 108"-wide fabric, use 1¾ yards (1 yard, 1⅝ yard, 2⅝ yards).*

Binding fabric: ⅝ yard (¼ yard, ½ yard, ¾ yard)

Batting: 63" x 75" (34" x 35", 55" x 58", 94" x 102")

PREPARATION

Copy full-size template (see pullout) onto template plastic or cardstock, copying all notes onto templates. Separate templates into arcs at line.

CUTTING INSTRUCTIONS

From background fabric, cut 16 (4, 16, 48) 11" squares.

From appliqué fabric(s), cut 16 (4, 16, 48) 10" squares.

ASSEMBLY

Fold and press appliqué squares in half once diagonally.

Align template at corner. Mark curves. Alternate between A through D templates, mixing and matching pieces but always making sure to include one outer ring for each block.

You may choose to omit or include center rings; the design works out either way.

Cut along each of the marks creating the rings.

ASSEMBLE BLOCKS

Using needle-turn appliqué (page 120), baste and sew cut arcs onto background square.

 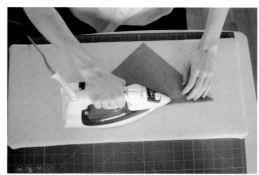 

ASSEMBLE QUILT TOP

Lay out finished blocks as shown in Figure 1, with 4 (2, 4, 6) columns across and 4 (2, 4, 8) rows down. Sew blocks together, pressing seams open where appliquéd edges meet. Press non-appliquéd edges in alternating directions so they nest (page 119).

Serging the edges: For the Railroad version, I serged all the edges after sewing the blocks together but before applying borders. I did this to keep the quilt top's raw edges clean. Denims fray, which can be exacerbated during the appliqué process. Because the denims are dark and I planned to apply white borders, I used a ⅜" seam allowance (to cover up my serging) and pressed the borders toward the blocks.

Refer to the Border Workshop (page 36) before attaching your borders.

Cut and attach a 12 1/2" (2 1/2", 4", 5") border at the top and a 12 1/2" (4", 4", 5") border at the bottom. Press seams toward border. Cut and attach 6 1/2" (2 1/2", 2 1/2", 11 1/2") borders at sides. Press seams toward border.

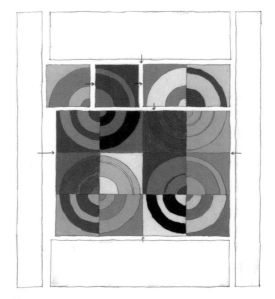

Figure 1

QUILT FINISHING

Baste and quilt as desired. Cut binding fabric into 7 (3, 5, 10) strips 2½" wide and see page 128 for finishing instructions.

BORDER WORKSHOP

When it comes to borders, there are a couple things to think about that will impact the final result. The first thing to consider is the pattern, weave or texture of fabric you will be using for the border. Is it directional?

If you are not using a directional fabric, go ahead and cut your borders in strips along the width of the fabric. If you need to attach multiple strips together to achieve the appropriate length, sew RIGHT sides *together*. A 45-degree-angled seam is usually less visible and will often result in a smoother transition, but it does use more fabric, which is why I often go with a straight-across seam. In either case, press the seam open after sewing.

When you use a directional fabric, you need to be a bit more careful when planning out your borders if you want the prints to be working in the same direction throughout (see page 74 Wasabi Trees for an example of directional borders). Of course, if having everything going in the same direction is not the look you are aiming for, then by all means use it as if the fabric were not directional; however, if you do want your borders to align, make sure you have extra fabric on hand for doing so. Next, instead of cutting each strip along the width of your fabric, plan your cuts so that each strip ends up working in the intended direction. I like doing this sometimes because it can truly unite the border and also add a fun little detail when you look at the quilt more closely. I encourage you to experiment with different options for each unique top you create.

The other important thing about borders is to determine how you want to attach them.

I often hesitate to list a specific length for a border in my patterns, because I know

Is your border fabric directional or non-directional?

that in reality the size of our finished quilt tops are likely to vary no matter how carefully we follow instructions. Many factors contribute to this, such as the seam allowance, the sewing foot, our specific machines, and the cutting tools we use. Trying to force a quilt top to fit pre-measured borders always makes for a quilting nightmare; the tops never lie flat and quilting becomes a huge challenge.

So let me teach you how to apply a border that fits your own top exactly.

The truth is that I never measure my borders when I am making a quilt. Instead, I cut and piece the strips together until I

have several more inches than I will need. To attach the borders to the quilt top, lay the border strip on the bottom (RIGHT side *up*) and the quilt top over it (RIGHT side *down*).

On a flat surface, pin them in place and sew along the edge, never pushing or pulling either part through.

Next, press the borders in the desired direction and take the top to your cutting table.

Lay your project flat, and use a ruler to trim the excess border to get a perfect right angle. This method works well for me every time!

SCALE

WHEN TALKING ABOUT SCALE, WE ARE TALKING ABOUT SIZE. There are three main areas where scale impacts the quilt: scale in the piecing, scale in the fabric itself, and scale in the quilting.

Scale is relative. The scale of each of these three main elements is dependent on how it relates to the surrounding design elements. The perception of the size of something is determined by how big (or small) the thing next to it is. All parts in your project put the other parts into perspective. Keep all these elements in check so that you can reach your goals.

As you work, evaluate what your goals are in terms of scale and how each element of your quilt contributes to that goal. When you start to get a handle on that, also consider contrast. When you use both together, you can do some pretty fun things with scale. For example, I love to use two fabrics next to each other that have low value contrast, but differ in scale. When you combine fabrics in this way, the composition has room to breathe and your eyes get an active experience. It may feel like your eyes are zooming in and out of a picture, or that your vision spreads after going small to big.

TIP: Think BIG and small when it comes to scale. Being deliberate about scale can bring depth and interest to your project.

Balancing scale will also help achieve a sense of depth in your designs. Tight and dense areas can hold your eye in, while larger motifs give your eye space to travel. Because of this, smaller scales can have the power to flatten and larger scales can convey depth. In a quilt, paying attention to the scale of the print on your fabric is one way to achieve that depth. The next project takes advantage of this, as well as piecing and quilting scale.

For the following Circle Lattice project, choose fabrics to play off the scale of the piecing, or audition a variety of fabric choices to create depth in the background or appliqué. Your quilting choices can also unify the scale of the fabrics and the piecing. Each of the project variations gives an example of how to achieve totally different visual effects by experimenting with the three main tools for establishing scale. These are great springboards for inspiring your own experimentation, depending on which effect you want to achieve in either my pattern or one of your own.

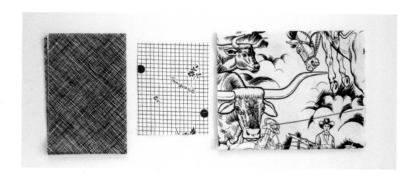

Scale is relative to
everything around it.

PROJECT | The design of this project takes advantage of multiple scales because of the two sizes of circles. The design also allows us to play with scale when we choose the fabric, and in how we decide to quilt it. When you see how I applied scale in fabric, piecing, and quilting in the variations, you will realize that there are many possible outcomes based on making intentional decisions about scale.

CIRCLE LATTICE

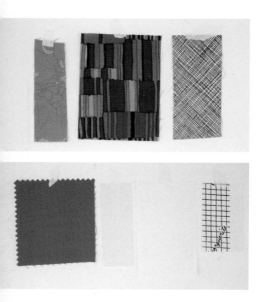

PLUM | big print on small texture

The Plum version uses a large-scale print for the appliqué and a small texture for the background. The nature of the appliqué fabric adds depth to this particular element of the design, and that is carried over by using that fabric in the borders as well. I mentioned before that it is fun to play with using fabrics within the same color range to achieve depth and interest in a design, and this version is a perfect example of how you can do that. It may seem counterintuitive, but when you maintain some consistency with your design choices, like with color, the differences (like scale) stand out even more.

FLAME | solids only

By using solid fabrics only, the shape of the appliqué itself has the most definition. Solids tend to read flat because of their uniform nature. Unless they have a pronounced weave, their biggest distinguishing factor is their color. Because there is no other surface competition, solid fabrics can be a showcase for pronounced quilting. This version of Circle Lattice (page 42) gives you a great opportunity to play with scale and dimension through your quilting.

COWBOY | big print meets big print

Many times, my designs stem from my curiosity about whether
something will work or not. This Cowboy variation is an example
of how two bold, large-scale fabrics can work to both express
the appliqué design as well as maintain each of their own
surface narratives. It is very tricky to find that balance; the
reason I thought these two could work together was because
of their high level of contrast. The cowboy print reads much
lighter in value because of the cream background, and the floral
print reads extremely dark because of the black background.
Because of that strong difference, there is less of a chance that
they will bleed together and get confusing. You can also use
this relationship to your advantage if you are trying to create a
softer look to the appliqué design itself. Using two bold prints
softens the contrast so that the appliqué design becomes
less noticeable. The design's boundary is also softened with a
scaled-down, texture in the border. Had I used a solid border
fabric, that boundary would be much harder.

Quilting can get lost in designs that involve two dominant prints,
or it can make the piece even more visually confusing. Unlike
with solids, the best solution for the quilting is not to fight with
the prints. I suggest an even, overall treatment. My focus in
this version was on the fabrics first, the appliqué motif second,
and then by default, the quilting comes in third. For a softer
approach, I used a coordinating thread (after some auditioning
I decided that cream blended in the best) and an even quilting
pattern (nothing but straight stuff here!). It is always about
decisions and priorities

TIP: Don't be afraid to
try something out. I
experiment all the time.
Some are hits, some
are misses, but all are
lessons learned. Most
everything can be sal-
vaged somehow; if not,
you can look forward
to moving on to the
next project with more
experience under your
belt. You can always
experiment with one
block before jumping
into the full project.
Take chances!

CIRCLE LATTICE

Finished Block Size: 33½" x 33½"

Finished Quilt Sizes: 40" x 42" wall, 83½" x 87½" full

Note: *Sizes are referred to in the following order: wall (full).*

MATERIALS
Background fabric(s): *1 yard (4 yards, can be cut into 1-yard increments for easier handling or if using multiple fabrics).*

Appliqué fabric(s): 1 yard (4 yards, can be cut into 1-yard increments for easier handling or if using multiple fabrics)

Border fabric: ½ yard (2½ yards)

Backing fabric: 2⅔ yards (7¾ yards)

Note: *For 108"-wide fabric, use 1½ yards (2⅝ yards)*

Binding fabric: *⅜ yard (¾ yard)*

Batting: 48" x 50" (92" x 96")

This whole-cloth appliqué technique is fun to work with, so try it out on a single-block wall quilt, and then graduate to a full-size quilt.

PREPARATION
Trace full-size template (see pullout) onto template plastic, freezer paper, or cardstock, copying all notes onto template.

CUTTING INSTRUCTIONS
From background fabric(s), cut 1 (4) 34" square(s).

From appliqué fabric(s), cut 1 (4) 34" square(s). Fold and press each square in half diagonally, three times to match the template shape.

I worked on a large cutting table pinning raw edges together to find the center line and then transported it to the ironing board to press.

Think BIG!: It can be tricky to work with large cuts of fabric. To ensure accurate alignment, fold, press, and then cut.

Transfer cut lines from template to appliqué fabric, aligning folds as indicated.

Pin through all layers before cutting to prevent layers from shifting during the process.

Cut along marked lines, moving pins as needed.

Transfer appliqué carefully to background fabric, unfold, taking out the pins as you go, and re-pinning the two layers into place once the appliqué is correctly positioned.

ASSEMBLE BLOCKS
Using needle-turn appliqué (page 120), baste and sew appliqué onto background square.

ASSEMBLE QUILT TOP

Lay out finished block as shown in Figure 1. For full-size top, lay out 2 columns across with 2 rows down.

Refer to the Border Workshop (page 36) before attaching your borders.

Cut and attach 3½" (8½") border for the top and 5½" (12½") border for the bottom. Press seams toward borders. Cut and attach 3½" (8½") borders at the sides. Press seams toward borders.

QUILT FINISHING

Baste and quilt as desired. Cut binding fabric into 5 (9) strips 2½" wide and see page 128 for finishing instructions.

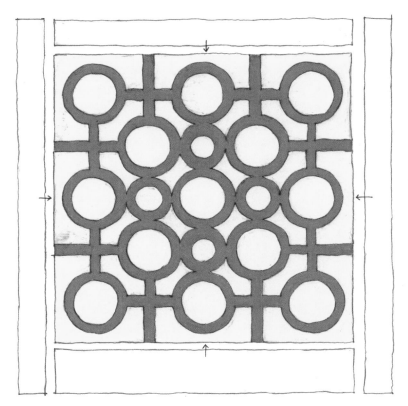

Figure 1

COLOR

COLOR IS EVERYTHING. Seriously. I am not exactly sure why it is, but no one can deny that color has a subjective impact on each of us. It is helpful to have a general understanding of color basics. You can use the terminology and concepts to think more logically about your projects and understand why you may be drawn to certain hues and shades more than others.

In familiarizing yourself with the language of color, you can start to be more discerning when choosing your own palettes. You will begin to pick up on subtleties and learn to be more intentional with your color selections.

While I always try to resolve any color issues through experimentation (with a fabric color card, paint chips, colored pencils, and markers), I also have a handful of resources I can tap into if I get really stuck. I recommend: Josef Albers, *Interaction of Color, Homage to the Square,* Wikipedia and Google.

Color inspiration can
be found everywhere.

WARM VS. COOL

On the most basic level, colors can be divided into two groups: warm and cool. Warm colors are typically yellow, red, and orange. Cool colors are generally blue, green, and purple.

The great (and sometimes confusing) thing about warm and cool colors is that there are warm and cool variants within each color group. This wide range of shades--or hues--gives us so much color goodness to work with. Look at the two shades of red below. Although red is generally considered to be a "warm color," the shade on the left is a cooler version with blue undertones. The shade on the right is a straight-up warm version with orangey-yellow undertones.

These differences can be subtle, but they are very important, especially when working with colors you do not normally use. For example, I generally stay away from using pink, but as the image below shows, there are many shades to work with. A warmer pink trending toward orange (shown on the right) is far more appealing to me than a cooler pink leaning toward purple.

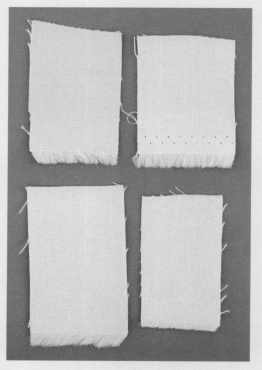

Kona Carnation (top left), Kona Peony (top right), Ice Peach (lower left), Dusty Peach (lower right)

Kona Tangerine (left) and Kona Lipstick (right)

Once you begin to really look at colors, you will get better at recognizing these differences, too. The best way to break out of any bias you have against a color is to audition a selection of shades and hues in your next project.

SATURATION AND VALUE

Another basic element of color to consider is the saturation and value of a hue. Hue is the pure color, like blue. Adjusting saturation and value creates navy, a variation of that hue.

Saturation is the color's level of intensity. How orange is that orange? Is it screaming or is it silent? The lowest saturation is the dullest version of a color created by the addition of black or gray to the hue.

Do not confuse saturation with value. A color with a low value (lighter with white added to the hue) can still be very saturated, just as a color high in value (darker with black or gray added to the hue) can have a low saturation.

If you are working on a quilt and love your color palette but overall the design is a bit flat, adjusting the saturation of one or more of the colors will help add depth and visual interest. You can use this to your advantage to guide the eye across the composition of the quilt and to create the intended feeling or mood.

These swatches show low value/low saturation (Kona Celery, bottom right), low value/high saturation (Kona Cactus, bottom left), high value/ low saturation (Kona Windsor, top right), and high/ value high saturation (Kona Oasis, top left).

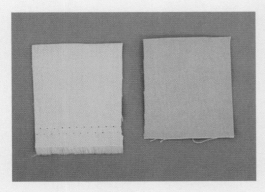

Kona Schoolbus (left), Kona Amber (right) showing that colors of similar value can have differing levels of saturation.

GETTING PERSONAL WITH COLOR

The next thing to understand about color is our subjective connection to it. I think it is a safe bet to guess that you had a favorite color as a kid. We all did. Color makes an impact on us at an early age. You also might associate certain colors with certain moods, or you are at least aware of societal associations with certain colors. Red might equate rage or power, whereas blue might convey calm. Or, turquoise might just be your favorite color, and it makes you sublimely happy because it reminds you of the beautiful waters at your favorite vacation spot. You might not even realize why you are drawn to a specific color. Either way, the connection is there. When working with color and choosing fabrics, being mindful of this connection can be personally illuminating.

When I was a kid, my favorite color was pink. Everything was pink. I mean, really, everything. I think that is the reason there is not very much pink in my life as an adult. Aside from the warmer shades mentioned earlier, I just never work with it. Other colors strike me now, and some of them I have a hard time getting away from. Flame, blue, and citron come to mind when I think of colors that I am currently using over and over.

We all get into certain color moods for short and long periods of time. These are colors that get in your mind for a few months or years and work their way into everything. It is like when you go to the store to buy a few things and later you realize that everything you bought not only is in the same few shades, but it also all matches. That happens to me all the time.

I am not sure exactly why we do this, but I will bet it is because of a mixture of things swirling around in our lives that includes (but is not limited to) our emotions and our surroundings. Thinking about a timeline and story to illustrate it, the color story comes immediately to mind

PERCEPTION AND INTUITION

Our perception of color depends on two things: how our eyes translate the color and the conditions under which we view it. For example, a deep plum color looks different when seen under indoor lighting in the evening versus natural light in the early morning. The appearance will change even more depending on the surface and the way the texture absorbs and reflects light. The plum color will also look different when placed next to white versus being placed next to a navy, gray, or another shade of purple.

This all just means that there are a lot of factors at play when we see color.

The examples on the left show how the same color can be made to look different because of the color it is surrounded by. The examples on the right show the opposite—two different colors can look the same by the colors they are surrounded by.

During my first year in college, I was a student in the art school. Our curriculum was all about building a strong foundation on such basics as 2D/3D design and drawing. In my 2D design class, we spent a good chunk of time working with, looking at, and thinking about color. One project specifically opened my mind to the power of color.

The project had a few components to it; what I remember most was that we had to take the same color and put it into two scenarios that would make it look like two completely different colors. I was fascinated by how you could take one color and make it not look like itself. We also had to do the reverse and take two different colors and make them look like the same color by surrounding them with colors that would best do that.

That art-school exercise taught me the importance of context. Everything is relative to what is around it. That idea has really stuck with me.

CRAFTING A COLOR STORY

In quilt making, these lessons about color are particularly important to add continuity to your work. By thinking about the emotional impact colors have on us and the context in which we use them, we can start telling a story and creating a narrative in our quilts through our color choices and the colors we choose to avoid. Remember that making adjustments to the values of the saturation levels or even substituting in a color that you are not naturally drawn to can unlock a whole new way for the story to be told. Try not to discount that a certain fabric may work well with your design even if it is not your favorite in isolation. I encourage you to experiment and embrace those happy accidents you may encounter when auditioning fabrics or making a test block, so that you can repeat those color combinations/stories in a more intentional way in the final design. The three projects in this chapter and their variations are great places for you to start exploring your own color journey.

PROJECT ONE | While driving around my
town looking at some fantastic old houses,
I noticed one with this amazing screen door
paneling that resembled a sunrise. The screen
was framed by thin strips of wood on all sides
as well as pieces that radiated out from a
circular center. The sunrise has been a muse
of mine before, and this one immediately
intrigued me. Those delineated background
sections and pronounced circles stuck in my
mind. So I started sketching.

FACING EAST

COLOR | solid families

The first version of the project was translated very literally from this original sketch (see left). In this approach, I thought about color not as an overall narrative, but as groups of color families created by the blocks themselves.

Working with colored pencils, I mapped out the colors in each block and thought about how they fit together in a variety of combinations. I thought about subtle shifts in blues, as well as other types of combinations like grays with peach and citron. In the end, I was happy with the way it worked and translated the drawing block for block by matching Kona cottons to each piece using my color card.

The color story in this version is not so much an overall statement, but more of an exploration in putting smaller groups of colors together, which is exactly why it would be a good place to begin for anyone just starting to work with color. It is a hard version to mess up, because you can run as wild as you want with your rays and sashing fabric and the stories that go with them. The white portions will unite it all together.

If working with color is a challenge for you, Facing East is a good one to get your feet wet. One direction would be to select background fabrics (rays and sashing) using your favorite color as your main color muse. Then head off to your stash or favorite fabric store to find as many variations of that color as you can. Remember that even one color can have a variety of options because of all the variations in hue and saturation. Being mindful of hue and saturation will help you start to identify what makes each version of the color different.

Look for variety when selecting your fabrics, but also choose fabrics that you like. In the end, that will make you happier with the outcome. When selecting fabrics for your rays and sashing, look for neutrals choices, like cream, white, gray, or black that will set off and complement your background colors. Remember the other tools that you have picked up so far, like contrast. Make sure there is a sufficient amount of contrast to showcase the design.

WHITE | relative color

As I have mentioned, color is relative. This is especially true when there is almost no color at all. In fact, with a limited palette like this, other design components can become more of a statement. Holding back on one element can result in a powerful emphasis on another.

In this version, you achieve color by way of a lack of color. In an environment of whites, creams, and grays, the subtle differences become even more pronounced. The whites feel whiter and the darks feel darker. Texture and subtlety become more evident elements in designs featuring a limited color range because there's not as much competition for the eye's attention color-wise. You can play up that design element by using a variety of types of fabric, such as corduroy, linen, and silk in combination with quilting cottons or voile.

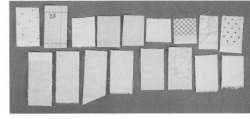

Using paper piecing to stabilize fabrics: Paper piecing makes working with multiple substrates very manageable, because the paper stabilizes the various types of fabric. For example, silk can have a much higher drape or tendency to flow compared with corduroy, which has a much more structured body. By using paper piecing to integrate these types of trickier fabrics, many of those differences are equalized.

When working with a more limited or subtle palette, it is usually a good idea to audition your fabric selections. This can be as easy as setting swatches of each fabric on the floor or design wall and seeing how it looks. Are all of the fabrics reading the same? Is there good variety? Is one fabric popping more than it should? Next, revisit your goals for the project. Will these fabrics create the look and feel you're aiming for? Try timing yourself so you don't get bogged down by too many options. After fifteen minutes of auditioning/playing/sorting, stop analyzing and jump into the project. Lay out the blocks as you are making them to ensure the project is still on track. Step back and evaluate your progress from a distance. You can always make adjustments as you go if you notice that there is too much of something here and not enough of something there.

CRANE | fussy cut focal in monochrome

Using a monochromatic (single) color palette, block distinction can come from several places—from the print scale, from the texture, or from the quilting. When evaluating a composition, your eye wants to highlight what is different about the given scenario. In a neutral palette with like colors, you notice a shift in the print on the fabric and the way it is quilted. Have fun playing with these layers if choosing a neutral, low volume or monochromatic color palette.

In this version of Facing East, I chose a small, textured gray print for the background pieces, a larger-scale gray print for the rays and sashing, and a special motif fabric for the circle center. With each selection from ray to circle center, the fabrics get darker and the print scale becomes larger. I did this so that there would be distinction between the sections, but also to create depth and to highlight new layers of the piecing. I chose the largest and darkest print for the circle center in order to really separate the circle from the piecing behind it. To further emphasize that contrast, the fabrics in the rest of the block are grays, and they've been quilted heavily and evenly to further unite them.

In this sketch on the left, you can see how over a larger quilt the circles could become portholes to tell that story.

FACING EAST

Finished Block Size: 10½" x 21"

Finished Quilt Sizes: 53" x 70½" throw, 11" x 25½" runner, 36" x 47½" wall/baby, and 84½" x 91½" full/queen

Note: *Sizes are referred to in the following order: throw (runner, wall/baby, full/queen).*

MATERIALS

Fabric A (rays and sashing): 4 yards total (⅜ yard, 1⅝ yards, 8¼ yards) or 92 (6, 36, 195) 1½" strips

Fabric B (background): 4¼ yards total (⅓ yard, 1¾ yards, 9 yards) or 60 (4, 24, 128) 2½" strips

Note: *Use assorted colors or a single color depending on the project.*

Fabric C (circle center): ⅝ yard (¼ yard, ¼ yard, ⅞ yard)

Border fabric: ½ yard (⅛ yard, ½ yard, ¾ yard)

Backing fabric: 3½ yards (⅝ yard, 2½ yards, 7¾ yards)

Note: *For 108"-wide fabric, use 1¾ yards (⅝ yard, 1¼ yards, 2⅝ yards).*

Binding fabric: ⅝ yard (¼ yard, ⅜ yard, ¾ yard)

Batting: 61" x 79" (19" x 34", 44" x 56", 93" x 100")

PREPARATION

Make 30 (2, 12, 64) copies each of Block Templates A and M (see pullout). This project requires 60 (4, 24, 128) blocks total.

CUTTING INSTRUCTIONS

From Fabric A, cut 1½" strips as needed to piece the blocks as noted on block template.

From Fabric B, cut 2½" strips as needed to piece the blocks as noted on block template.

From Fabric C, cut 15 (1, 6, 32) circles using Facing East circle template (see pullout) by first cutting 15 (1, 6, 32) 6" square(s). Press in half and then in half again.

Align template with quarter folds. Mark and cut out the circles. Do not press flat after cutting. You will be using fold lines as reference for further alignment.

ASSEMBLE BLOCKS

Working from strips, paper piece blocks (page 127). After completing each block, staystitch ¼" along arcs edge to stabilize curve.

ASSEMBLE QUILT TOP

Lay out finished block templates as shown in Figure 1, with 10 (2, 6, 16) columns across and 6 (2, 4, 8) rows down.

Making the Block Units

Sew together four-unit blocks along solid seam lines.

Remove paper in seam allowance after each seam. Press seams open.

Carefully remove and recycle all remaining paper and press.

Attaching the Circle

Align pressed folds with block seams.

Baste in place and then use needle-turn appliqué to attach (page 120). Doing this step on a flat surface is key to keeping your block flat.

ASSEMBLING THE BLOCKS

Lay out finished blocks as shown with 5 (1, 3, 8) columns across and 3 (1, 2, 4) rows down. Sew blocks together to finish layout, pressing seams so they nest (page 119)

Refer to the Border Workshop (page 36) before attaching your borders.

Cut and attach 4" (2½", 3", 4") borders at top and bottom. Press seams toward borders. For wall/baby size, also cut and attach 2½" borders at sides. Press seams toward borders.

QUILT FINISHING

Baste and quilt as desired. Cut binding fabric into 7 (2, 5, 9) strips 2½" wide and see page 128 for finishing instructions.

Figure 1

PROJECT TWO | Having grown up in the Florida citrus country, I am very familiar with being surrounded by orange groves. I have always loved aerial views, especially those of the areas where I grew up. There is something enticingly beautiful about the long, orderly rows of trees that form a grid of assorted sizes of circles from above. The design for this quilt is inspired by those shapes and that rhythm.

AERIAL GROVE

GRADATION | changing color

You can also craft a color story in your work through a color-changing gradation. For example, at the top of this quilt, the fabrics are blue. By the time you get to the bottom, the blocks have changed from green to blue to purple to red to orange to yellow. The color relationship among the blocks transitions from the starting point to something totally different. Creating a color gradation can make a bold and beautiful statement.

The fabric pull is sometimes the most enjoyable part of a project; this one was especially gratifying for me, because I knew I wanted to create a color gradation. When doing this, it is important to also decide upon and control the pace and flow of that change.

For those of you who love little bits of a lot of different fabrics, this version of Aerial Grove is for you. It has no fabric repeats. I raided my stash for a plethora of 2½" squares that in general hold a strong color position.

Take a small cutting mat, rotary cutter, and a ruler into your stash and just start hacking away. As you cut 2½" squares, lay each piece side-by-side in color order so you can see exactly how the variety is shaping up. If you are comparing fabrics at a store, grab fat quarters or eighths or bolts and find a space to lay them out so you can assess how your color gradation is coming together. Try not to get attached to any one transition while you are building your palette. Sometimes the trick might be to change the order of things so that it works out better.

For the background, choose something that will showcase your color gradation well. Keep in mind that the background you chose will have to work with a wide range of fabrics. It is okay for your background to blend with some of the scraps, as long as your overall statement is being expressed

For my version, I wanted a variety of whites and creams in the background. I imagined the pieces of background as plots of land, and I knew from the beginning that I would use the subdivided background pieces as quilting zones.

Creating smooth gradation: Fabrics that hold a strong color position are those that, even though it might be a print, are dominantly one color. Using fabrics such as this is essential for creating a smooth transition in your color gradation.

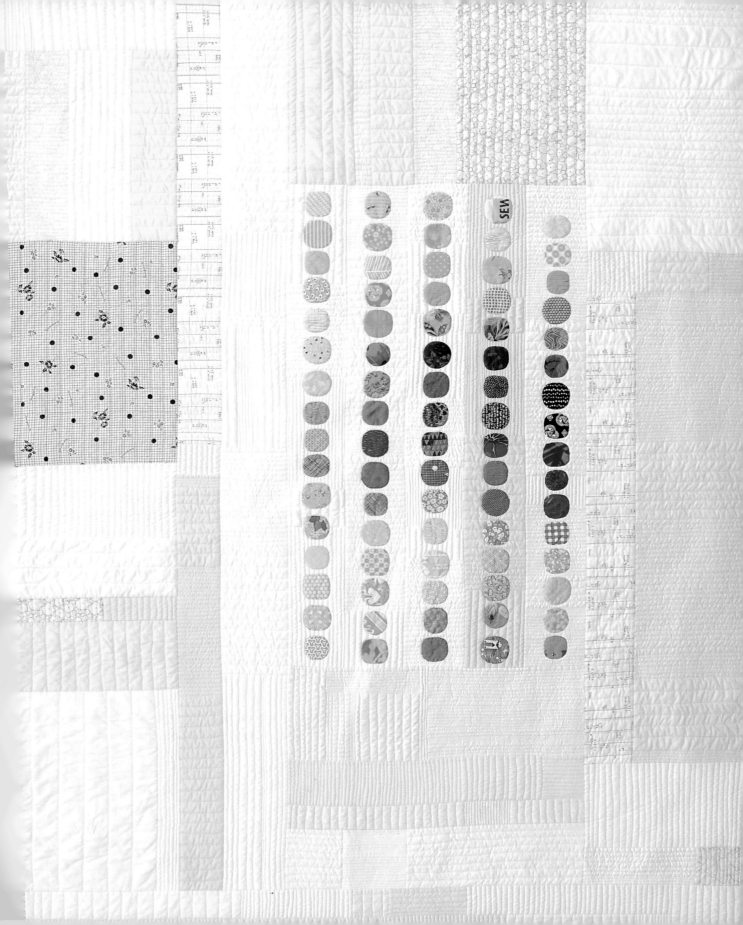

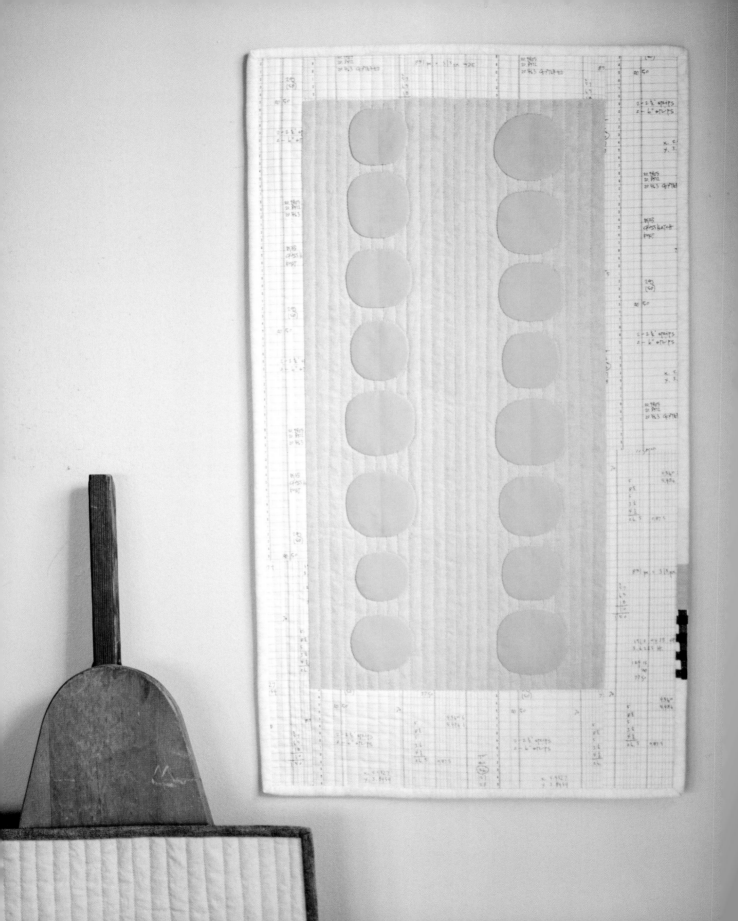

WASABI | single fabric trees

Because of the variety of colors and fabrics in the appliqués in the Gradation version, the subtle differences in their appliqué shapes become less obvious. The fabrics in this Wasabi version play with texture (mix of substrates), print (solid vs. print), and line. But by using the same color for the appliquéd trees, the irregularity of the circles is emphasized. In any design, you as the maker choose what to emphasize and how you want to do it. There are no wrong decisions, just different choices leading to their own results. This is a great project for fussy cutting and playing I-Spy with your favorite fabrics or motifs.

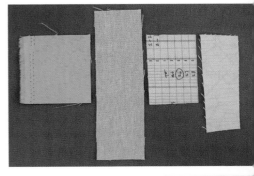

Adding a scrappy binding: You can always spice up the binding by adding in a scrap or two of a different fabric. Because of the limited and orderly palette in this particular project, I felt that the binding should be having a little fun of its own.

AERIAL GROVE

Finished Quilt Sizes: 83½" x 88½" full/
queen, 14½" x 26" runner, 42½" x 42" wall,
66½" x 76½" throw

Note: *Sizes are referred to in the following
order: full/queen (runner, wall, throw)*

MATERIALS
Appliqué background fabric(s): 1 yard
(¼ yard, 1 yard, 1 yard)

Appliqué fabrics (assorted colors):
80 (16, 80, 80) 2½" squares (or ½ yard
[⅛ yard, ½ yard, ½ yard] of a single color)

**Border fabric (cuts to equal overall
amount):** 5¼ yards, ⅜ yard, ¾ yard,
3½ yards)

Note: *More yardage is required for
directional prints.*

Backing fabric: 7¾ yards, ¾ yard, 2⅞ yards,
4¾ yards)

Note: *For 108"-wide fabric, use 2⅝ yards
(⅝ yard, 1½ yards, 2 ⅛ yards).*

Binding fabric: ¾ yard (¼ yard, ⅜ yard,
⅝ yard)

Batting: 92" x 97" (23" x 34", 51" x 50",
75" x 85")

CUTTING INSTRUCTIONS
From appliqué background fabric(s), cut 5
(2, 5, 5) 5½" x 42" (21", 42", 42") strips.

From appliqué fabrics, cut 80 (16, 80, 80)
2½" squares.

APPLIQUÉ
Fold and press each appliqué square in
half and in half again to create a quarter
fold.

Using sharp appliqué scissors, cut quarter-
folded piece along raw edges into an arc.

Each circle is unique, so do not worry
about getting perfect circles or identical
sizes.

ASSEMBLE ROWS
Fold and press appliqué background strips
in half lengthwise to mark center. Position
cut circles by aligning center circle fold
with center strip fold.

Using needle-turn appliqué (page 120),
baste and sew circles onto each appliqué
background strip.

ASSEMBLE QUILT TOP
Lay out rows as shown in Figure 1, so that
the 5 (2, 5, 5) rows are long sides together.
Sew rows together, pressing seams in
a consistent direction. The borders are
created by sewing together many smaller
pieces of fabric of varying heights and
widths until the correct size is achieved
(page 132). Beginners might consider

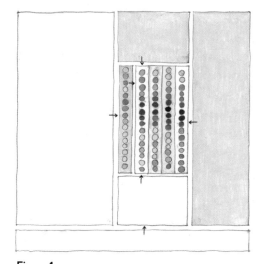

Figure 1

  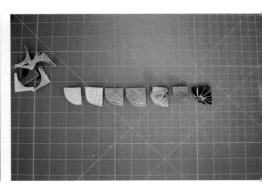

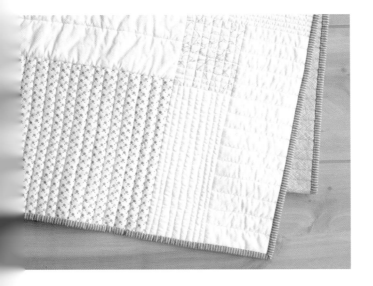

cutting the borders to size (page 132) from yardage rather than piecing.

Refer to the Border Workshop (page 36) before attaching your borders.

QUILT FINISHING

Baste and quilt as desired. Cut binding fabric into 9 (3, 5, 8) strips 2½" wide and see page 128 for finishing instructions.

LEFT: I pieced the borders this way in anticipation of how I wanted to quilt it. Sewing together smaller pieces of fabric breaks up the large border area and provides areas for me to change up my quilting stitches.

PROJECT THREE | My sewn stationery is admittedly kind of a non-project in terms of skill, preparation, and supplies, but that is also the beauty of it. The idea originally grew out of my love of handwritten notes, mixed with the reality that I am not usually prepared to write and send one. A proponent of improvising on the fly and working with what you have, I am always ready to put one of these guys together with no more than a sheet of plain cardstock (of which I always keep a healthy supply) and some fabric scraps. The best thing about this project is that it allows you to play with fabric combos quickly and without too much thinking or planning. Part of the fun is seeing what comes out of the scrap pile, and it's even more of a surprise to find great and interesting combinations that you wouldn't have thought of otherwise.

SEWN STATIONERY

When honing your skills on just about anything, practice is key, and learning how to put fabrics and colors together is no different. Whether you are a seasoned mixer or you have a low comfort level for it, this project will warm you up to new ideas and encourage you to think and act quickly on your feet. I find that just half an hour of making these cards works wonders! You stop being precious, and you start thinking in an open way. This then leads to new inspiration for your other projects.

Constraints and limitations can be great. They eliminate the feeling of being overwhelmed and force you to come up with a creative solution. I am grateful for limitations; it's empowering to know you can create a color story from your stash and just the scraps of fabric you have on hand. Most of us don't have an endless supply of the "perfect" fabrics at our disposal. I am sometimes happy not to have a fabric shop within close range because it forces me to find a design solution using whatever I have. When you are given the chance to improvise with very little risk, you often end up with some very inspiring results. Plus, by exploring the possibilities in your stash first you will save you the travel time to the store that you can now use for sewing. I'm all about maximizing that. Less time pushing the gas pedal equals more time pushing the sewing pedal.

Just to get you started, here are some ideas for working from your scrap pile.

1. Begin by coordinating scraps from projects in this book or projects that you have already made. This is an easy place to start—your pairings have already been decided.

2. Try to create a monochromatic palette from what you have lying around. Do you have a lot of one color? Start grouping like things. Put them all together and see how rich and diverse they look.

3. To push yourself, grab two crazy fabrics that you would never put together otherwise and see if there is a unifying element you could highlight so they can start speaking to each other. Sometimes this could be as simple as finding a solid that complements them both. As you get better with this, work on bridging three wild ones by creating a hierarchy between them and finding a way to highlight the language they all speak.

4. Once you've got the hang of the above approaches, push your skills further by blindly reaching into your scrap bin and pulling something out. Being able to handle surprises becomes empowering, and it is exciting to know you can make nice with anything that gets thrown your way. Plus, it is fun not knowing what is next!

SEWN STATIONERY

SUPPLIES
Fabric scraps of any size.

Cardstock: I like A6, A2, and 4Bar sizes. Usually flat stock is my preference, but if you want more area to work and write on, you can choose a folded format in these sizes. See Resources (page 144).

SEWING INSTRUCTIONS
Arrange your scraps on your cutting mat. Select fabrics and place on the cardstock

Lengthen sewing machine stitch length to 3.0mm. Load sewing machine with coordinating thread (contrasting thread could be fun, too!). Stitch fabric swatches in place and trim threads.

Leaving enough space: Keep in mind where you'll be writing your note when placing your fabric and planning your stitches. Since I am most often using flat stock, I usually position the fabric to one side to allow for a chunk of space to write my note.

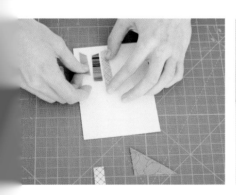

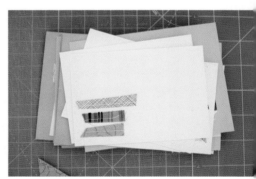

EMPHASIS

EMPHASIS IS ALL ABOUT MAKING A THOUGHTFUL DECISION ABOUT HOW TO BRING YOUR DESIGN TO LIFE. Through fabric placement, quilting intention, and all of the other tools explored in this book, you can create emphasis by highlighting different parts of a design. Why not control the outcome as much as you can?

Here's an example to think about. Maybe you want to make a quilt inspired by the shape of the waves in the ocean. You already have the perfect shape in your mind, you've picked out your fabrics, and you have come up with a solution for making the shape. Now you need to determine the visual impact you want it to make. When making a quilt, you are in full control of bringing your idea to life. Maybe the reason you are drawn to the idea of a wave is because of the shape itself, or maybe it is because of the way the wave blends into the rest of the water as it washes on shore. These two scenarios are very different. In the first, you may want the shape of the wave to be most prominent, and therefore that is what you will plan to emphasize. In the second, you are likely more interested in the environment in which the wave functions, and to re-create that you will be emphasizing the system as a whole first and the wave itself second. In both of these scenarios, emphasis is your friend.

TIP: What is the most important thing that you want to say in your project? Being deliberate about emphasis makes your message clear.

The quilt block is a pretty amazing animal. In the example above, I highlighted just two ways you could take the same inspiration and design to create different results. Here is another example. Think about all the different variations and effects you can achieve with the classic log cabin block. In addition to the standard grid layout, you can create a zigzag, a diagonal strip, floating sections, something super minimal, the list goes on…. What makes each outcome different is how you manipulate your block to create emphasis.

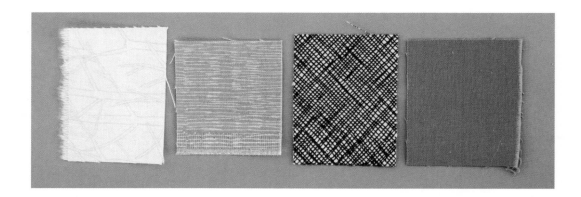

PROJECT | The following project explores the idea of emphasis. I've taken one block and created three variations, simply by placing the fabrics in different positions on the block. I kicked up the challenge by working with the same four fabrics in each version. Imagine how different these blocks could be by also changing the fabrics!

EMPHASIS

EMPHASIS | stripe

In this first version, I used the block to create a stripe. In order to do this, I mirrored the original block and placed my fabric so that like fabrics would meet at the block edges and therefore stretch across the project to create a stripe. Quilting these like sections together further emphasizes that aspect of the design.

EMPHASIS | medallion

By placing the fabrics in new positions, I created a medallion motif in the second version. Instead of meeting like fabrics at the block edges, I contained the fabrics within their own sections. I quilted around these areas to further highlight the medallion shapes and textures.

EMPHASIS | fringe

The final block is certainly a departure from the first two versions. To move the design out and into the borders, I used two different fabric placement strategies for the blocks, negative space by way of a whole-cloth section in the center, and additional borders on the top and bottom. The quilting then plays off the texture in the fabric in the center, giving it an even and consistent, overall feel. I limited the quilting in the cream and spice areas so they would pop; then I introduced new, more spacious texture in the top and bottom sections to allow for more body.

STRIPE

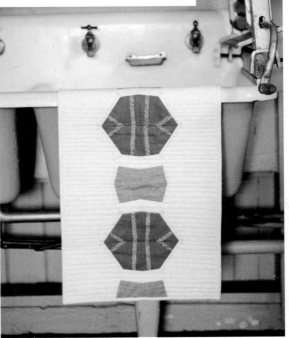

MEDALLION

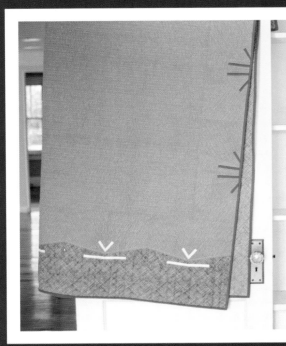

FRINGE

EMPHASIS

Finished Block Size: 6½" x 8"

Finished Quilt Sizes: 16½" x 39½" runner, 39½" x 48½" wall/baby, 65½" x 75½" throw

Note: *Sizes are referred to in the following order: runner (wall/baby, throw).*

MATERIALS: STRIPE
Fabric A: ¼ yard (½ yard, 1 yard)

Fabric B: 1 yard (2½ yards, 5½ yards)

Fabric D: ⅜ yard (⅞ yard, 1⅝ yard)

MATERIALS: MEDALLION
Fabric A: ⅜ yard (⅞ yard, 1⅝ yard)

Fabric B: ⅛ yard (⅜ yard, ⅝ yard)

Fabric C: ⅛ yard (⅜ yard, ¾ yard)

Fabric D: 1 yard (2⅜ yards, 3¾ yards)

MATERIALS: FRINGE
Fabric A: 0 yards (⅛ yard, ⅛ yard)

Fabric B: ½ yard (½ yard, 1⅛ yard)

Fabric C: 1 yard (2¾* yard, 5½* yards)

*This measurement includes yardage for the quilt center.

Fabric D: ⅛ yard (⅛ yard, ¼ yard)

ADDITIONAL MATERIALS: ALL VERSIONS
Backing fabric: 1⅜ yards (2¾ yards, 4¼ yards)

Note: *For 108"-wide fabric, use ¾ yard (1½ yards, 2⅛ yards).*

Binding fabric: ¼ yard (⅜ yard, ⅝ yard)

Batting: 25" x 48" (48" x 57", 74" x 84")

STRIPE

PREPARATION
Make 6 (18, 40) copies of each Block Template A and M (pages 138, 139). This project requires 12 (36, 80) blocks total.

CUTTING INSTRUCTIONS

STRIPE FABRIC CUTTING CHART
Cut sequentially: Strips will be subcut

+ From fabric A, cut 4" strips.
+ From fabric B, cut 9¼" strips.
+ From fabric D, cut 1½" and 2" strips.

	FABRIC	SIZE	QUANTITY
1	A	1¼"×4"	12 (36, 80)
2	D	1½"×4"	12 (36, 80)
3	D	1½"×4"	12 (36, 80)
4	D	2"×3"	12 (36, 80)
5	A	3½"×2½"	12 (36, 80)
6	D	1½"×3¼"	12 (36, 80)
7	B	3½"×3¼"	12 (36, 80) use scrap from #10
8			
9	D	1½"×2½"	12 (36, 80)
10	B	9¼" wide×8" tall	12 (36, 80)

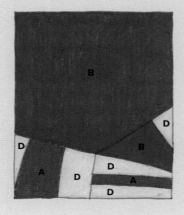

ASSEMBLE BLOCKS

Paper piece blocks by size. See paper piecing instructions on page 123.

Note: On each quilt block, adjacent pieces in the same fabric are pieced as one section, not individually. These are shown on the Cutting Chart as a grouping of numbered pieces with a single cut fabric piece.

ASSEMBLE QUILT TOP

Lay out finished blocks as shown in Figure 1, with 6 (6, 10) columns across and 2 (6, 8) rows down. Sew together along solid seam lines. Remove paper in seam allowance after each seam. Press seams so they nest (page 119).

Carefully remove and recycle all remaining paper.

QUILT FINISHING

For Throw version only, refer to the Border Workshop (page 36) before attaching your borders.

Cut and attach 6" borders for the top and bottom. Press seams toward borders. Baste and quilt as desired. Cut binding fabric into 3 (5, 8) strips 2½" wide and see page 128 for finishing instructions.

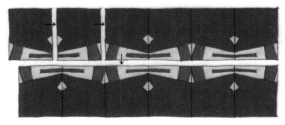

Figure 1

MEDALLION

PREPARATION

Make 6 (18, 40) copies of each Block Template A and M (pages 138, 139). This project requires 12 (36, 80) blocks total.

CUTTING INSTRUCTIONS

MEDALLION FABRIC CUTTING CHART
Cut sequentially: Strips will be subcut

+ From fabric A, cut 4" strips.
+ From fabric B, cut 1¼" strips.
+ From fabric C, cut 3" strips.
+ From fabric D, cut 9¼" strips.

	FABRIC	SIZE	QUANTITY
1	B	1¼"×4"	12 (36, 80)
2	A	1½"×4"	12 (36, 80)
3	A	1½"×4"	12 (36, 80)
4	D	2"×3"	12 (36, 80) use scrap from #10
5	C	3½"×3"	12 (36, 80)
6			
7	B	1¼"×3"	12 (36, 80)
8	A	1½"×2½"	12 (36, 80) use scrap from #10
9	A	3"×3¼"	12 (36, 80)
10	D	9¼" wide×8" tall	12 (36, 80)

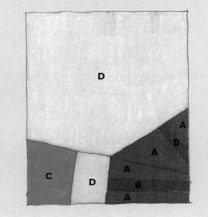

ASSEMBLE BLOCKS

Paper piece blocks by size. See paper piecing instructions on page 123.

Note: On each quilt block, adjacent pieces in the same fabric are pieced as one section, not individually. These are shown on the Cutting Chart as a grouping of numbered pieces with a single cut fabric piece.

ASSEMBLE QUILT TOP

Lay out finished blocks as shown in Figure 2 with 6 (6, 10) columns across and 2 (6, 8) rows down. Sew together along solid seam lines. Remove paper in seam allowance after each seam. Press seams so they nest (page 119).

Carefully remove and recycle all remaining paper.

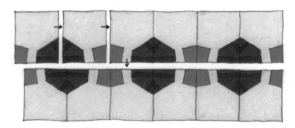

Figure 2

QUILT FINISHING

For Throw version only, refer to the Border Workshop (page 36) before attaching your borders.

Cut and attach 6" borders for the top and bottom. Press seams toward borders. Baste and quilt as desired. Cut binding fabric into 3 (5, 8) strips 2½" wide and see page 128 for finishing instructions.

FRINGE

PREPARATION

The Fringe throw and wall/baby sizes have blocks only along the edges. For these versions, first cut 3 yards from Fabric C and piece center to 52½" by 48½" for throw or first cut 1 yard from Fabric C and trim to 26½" x 32½" for wall/baby prior to cutting fabric for the blocks per the Fabric Cutting Chart.

Make 6 (10, 16) copies of each Block Template A and M (pages 138, 139). This project requires 12 (20, 32) blocks total.

CUTTING INSTRUCTIONS

See Fabric Cutting Chart (right).

ASSEMBLE BLOCKS

Paper piece blocks by size. See paper piecing instructions on page 123.

Note: On each quilt block, adjacent pieces in the same fabric are pieced as one section, not individually. These are shown on the Cutting Chart as a grouping of numbered pieces with a single cut fabric piece.

ASSEMBLE QUILT TOP

Lay out finished blocks as shown in Figure 3, with 6 (6, 10) columns across and 2 (6, 8) rows down around the center fabric for throw and wall/baby sizes. Sew together along solid seam lines. Remove paper in seam allowance after each seam. Press seams so they nest (page 119).

Carefully remove and recycle all remaining paper.

FRINGE FABRIC CUTTING CHART
Cut sequentially: Strips will be subcut

(top/bottom blocks)
+ From fabric B, cut 4" strips.
+ From fabric C, cut 9¼" strips.
+ From fabric D, cut 1¼"

	FABRIC	SIZE	QUANTITY
1	D	1¼"×4"	12 (12, 20)
2	B	1½"×4"	12 (12, 20)
3	B	1½"×4"	12 (12, 20)
4			
5	B	3½"×4"	12 (12, 20)
6			
7	D	1¼"×3"	12 (12, 20)
8	C	1½"×2½"	12 (12, 20) use scrap from #10
9	C	3"×3¼"	12 (12, 20) use scrap from #10
10	C	9¼" wide ·×8" tall	12 (12, 20)

(SIDE blocks)
+ From fabric C, cut 4" and 9¼" strips.
+ From fabric A, cut 1¼" strips.

	FABRIC	SIZE	QUANTITY
1	A	1¼"×4"	Ø (8, 12)
2	C	1½"×4"	Ø (8, 12)
3	C	1½"×4"	Ø (8, 12)
4			
5	C	3½"×4"	Ø (8, 12)
6			
7	A	1¼"×3"	Ø (8, 12)
8	C	1½"×2½"	Ø (8, 12) use scrap from #10
9	C	3"×3¼"	Ø (8, 12) use scrap from #10
10	C	9¼" wide ×8" tall	Ø (8, 12)

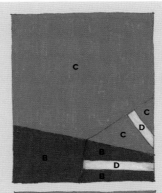

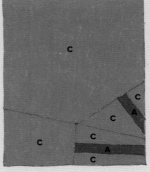

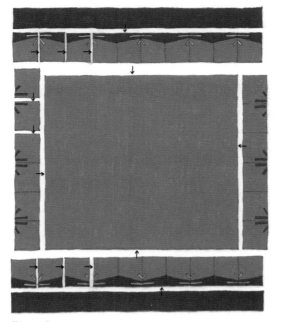

Figure 3

QUILT FINISHING

For Throw version only, refer to the Border Workshop (page 36) before attaching your borders.

Cut and attach 6" borders for the top and bottom. Press seams toward borders.

Baste and quilt as desired. Cut binding fabric into 3 (5, 8) strips 2½" wide and see page 128 for finishing instructions.

WHEN CONSIDERING VOLUME, THINK ABOUT THE WAYS TO EXPLORE PHYSICAL SPACE AND FORM IN YOUR QUILTS. Of course, volume can be used to describe other aspects of the quilt as well, such as the color or value range in a project, but here I am specifically exploring the physical distinction.

The opportunity of playing with that physical depth is a big reason why I think of quilt making as a serious upgrade from drawing. In a quilt, you can create form in addition to a sense of space within your project, by way of your materials and how you choose to use them. Elsewhere in this book I've talked about creating visual depth and space with tools such as line, contrast, scale, and color; here we are going to look at ways to build that physical depth and space with volume.

TIP: Physical space in quilting can be so much fun to explore. Construction, materials, and techniques all add volume to your projects.

Much of the volume in a quilt comes from the actual quilting itself, but you can enhance the physicality of a quilt during the piecing and fabric selection stages as well. For example, if you choose velveteen, corduroy, and other thick fabrics, they will provide much more physical mass than lighter fabrics like silk or voile would.

Your piecing strategy can also contribute. Appliqué builds volume as pieces of fabric are layered on top of each other to create your design. The way you press your seam allowances also creates differences in depth: pressing a seam open results in an even distribution of material behind the two pieces, while pressing to one side will add bulk to that side—a way of adding volume that many quilters don't consider. Pairing pressing direction with fabric selection can pack a double punch before ever getting to the next step, the quilting.

Functionally, quilting serves the purpose of holding the components of your project—the top, batting, and backing—together, but that is only the very beginning. Considering how to quilt your top (by machine or by hand?) and how densely to quilt it (close together or far apart?) is the first step. Quilting by machine compresses your project layers much more than if you choose to quilt by hand. Each of these strategies will make a big difference in the feel of the quilt.

The density of quilting is another big creator or eliminator of volume. Areas of high density quilting make areas of low or no density feel especially full and fluffy. When thinking about how densely or sparsely to quilt, consider the impact you want to create. For more enhanced and dramatic volume, employ a wider range of densities with your quilting. For less of a statement, keep your quilting more even.

BATTING

We can't talk about volume in quilts without talking about batting. That seems pretty obvious, right? The batting is how much meat we put between our top and bottom layers, and there are lots of options to choose from.

HIGH/LOW LOFT

The amount of loft in batting is basically an indication of how fluffy it is. High loft is thicker, and low loft is thinner, and they will contribute to your project as you would expect. What you may not expect is that lower loft batting can be easier to quilt, whereas higher loft can demand a little more attention and strategy in your quilting.

FIBER CONTENT MATTERS

The basic options in terms of fiber content are either synthetic (man-made, such as polyester) or natural (cotton, wool, and bamboo). It is not always the case that one particular fiber genre of batting is thick and another is thin, but you generally find cotton in lower-loft options; wool is on the higher side, and polyester runs the full

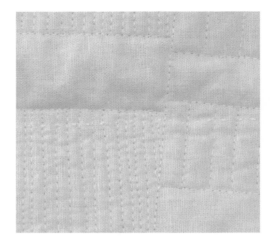

Employing various amounts of density in your quilting will lead to a variety of results in volume.

gamut. In the Map projects in this section, I chose wool batting because it is a natural fiber with high loft.

USING MULTIPLE LAYERS

Another batting option is to use multiple layers in your project. You don't want to get too carried away, but do give it a try if you are interested. I've started experimenting with using multiple layers of batting and am finding that you can get some great volume in doing so. In my Scrappy Bulls-eye, Colorful Aerial Grove, and the Blue and Gray Crazy sets (see the following Texture section), I used multiple layers of batting. One thing to consider is that depending on the batting you use and the size of your project, your quilt may get heavy. This can be a good thing or bad thing depending on your intent for the project. Multiple layers can also make it more difficult to quilt, but the results can be well worth it.

I know that the final step of quilting a top is a scary idea for a lot of people, and I can understand why. You spend a lot of time (and money) putting it together, and the quilting can be a very visible step. So here are a couple things for you to think about.

1. Don't be intimidated, but do be realistic: We see amazing quilting online, in magazines, in books, and at shows. It is important to remember that often the design we are most impressed by was created by someone who has spent years practicing and refining her or his skills. The good news is that you, too, can get your skills to that level by putting in time to practice—I promise! It is never realistic to expect that you will start out at the top. Instead, you should be absolutely encouraged to know that you will forever be improving each time you practice.

   If seeing other quilters' work is getting you down, it is time to put the blinders on and focus on how far you've come in your own quilt making journey. I guarantee that if you focus on the many steps you've overcome to get where you are, you'll start feeling pretty excited about how far that growth will continue to take you in the future.

2. Fancy equipment, schmancy equipment. It is true that having the right tools can make a task much easier. When it comes to quilting, you might think that you can't try or that you won't be any good because you don't have the perfect machine to quilt with. I won't deny that certain machines can make aspects of the quilt making process easier, but I will say that there are no shortcuts to learning the basics of quilting. Many of those basics can be learned on any machine, small or big. Don't have a machine? Not to worry, there's plenty to learn when quilting by hand too.

   Here's an example. When I made my very first quilt, I didn't think twice about tackling it using the very small machine I had at the time. It was the quilting that enticed me, and I couldn't wait to jump in and try it. The quilt I was working on was a very large throw that I did a horrible job of basting together (how was I to know the difference?), and I quilted it ridiculously densely, especially for a project that was my first time with free motion. But I did not care about any of that, and, the fact is, I had a great time doing it. I knew that it was opening a world of possibilities for my work and me. Knowing what I do now, I wouldn't choose to quilt something that big on a machine that small, but because I took that initial step and used what I had, I learned that I really liked the process, and I got the basics down and quickly figured out what direction I wanted to go in my quilting. If you are really determined to do something, find a way to do it.

3. Choosing fabric and thread will keep (or spill) your secrets. When just starting out, selecting a thread color that blends into the majority of the fabric will help make you feel more confident knowing that not every stitch is going to be showcased. The same is true when selecting your fabric. A solid will always showcase stitches prominently, while prints can allow your stitches to fade into them. The imperfections and mistakes that I made quilting my first quilt are not very noticeable, because of these two things. I worked with fairly loud prints, and the thread I used matched so well that it settles nicely into everything else. The fact that my bad basting job resulted in some pretty massive puckers in the back is almost impossible to notice without looking really closely because of the fabric I chose for the back.

Map print from
my Architexture
fabric collection

PROJECT | My Map project is perfect for exploring physical volume. As a whole-cloth project (meaning the top is created from a single, whole piece of fabric), the quilting design is the project. The inspiration for this particular project came from a design from my fabric collection Architextures, which was originally inspired by my drawing of a map of St. Louis that I created from one of my studies in architecture school. Over time, it has been fascinating for me to take the same series of lines from that original study and explore them in new and different ways. As a drawing, I drafted the lines carefully to study the way in which the grid was changing. On fabric, the ideas of color and repetition were introduced, and of course I had to use the fabric in a quilt. Now in this project, I took that same set of lines and quilted them to create the three-dimensional space that defines the design.

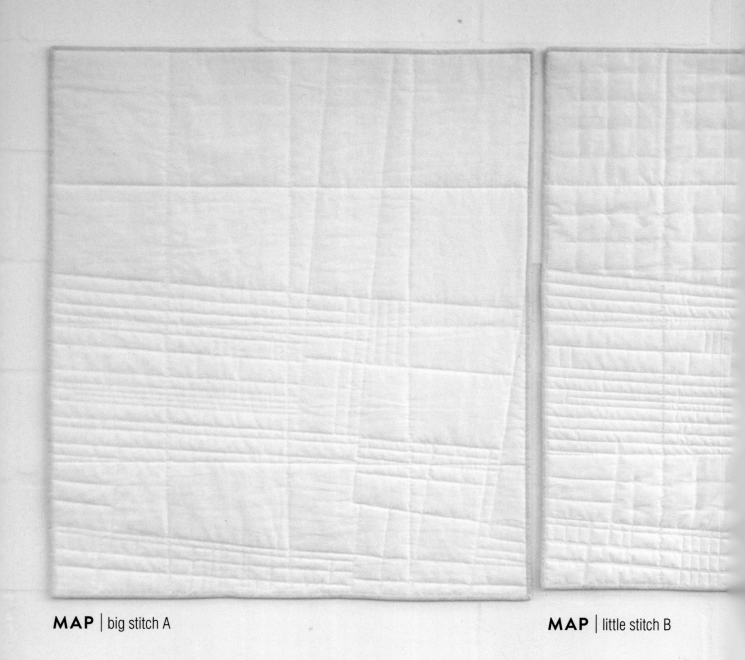

MAP | big stitch A

MAP | little stitch B

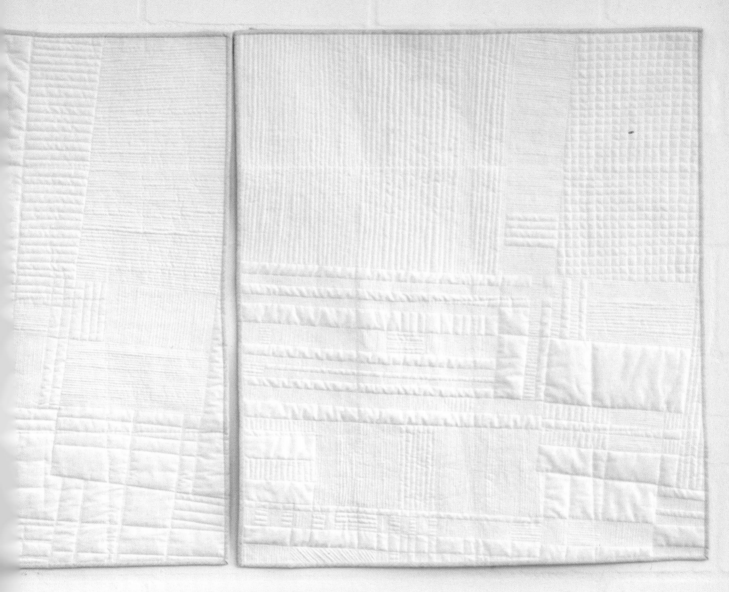

MAP | little stitch C

MAP

Finished Quilt Size: 34" x 40"

MATERIALS
Background fabric: 1 yard

Backing fabric: 1½ yards

Binding fabric: ⅜ yard

Batting: 42" x 48"

Note: *This is a whole-cloth project, which means that the design will be created with the quilting. I started with a plain piece of fabric on top and quilted the design right into it. Using a high-loft batting will add volume for a more dramatic effect. For all the versions I've created, I used wool batting because of its high loft. This quilt features Essex Linen from Robert Kaufman, which has a sturdy texture and quilts up beautifully.*

Wool batting, Ivory Essex linen, No 8. perle cotton, 50 wt. cotton thread

PREPARATION
Cut background fabric to 34" x 40". Fold along the dotted lines as shown in Figures 1, 2, and 3 and press background panel so that guides are in place for transferring map template guidelines. Make all folds on one side at a time, accordion-style. Unfold fabric. Using removable marking tool (see Resources section on page 144), transfer all map base lines (on page 133) to background panel by using fold lines as reference points. Don't worry about getting each line absolutely perfect. The goal is to approximate the lines where you need them as best as you can. I guarantee no one will know the difference if it is a bit off.

ASSEMBLE QUILT TOP
Baste marked top panel, batting, and backing fabric together.

QUILT FINISHING
Quilt along marked lines. Use additional quilting as desired to create even more volume. I also mixed big-stitch hand quilting with machine quilting. Explore your options and have fun with making the map your own. Cut binding fabric into 4 strips 2½" wide and see page 128 for finishing instructions.

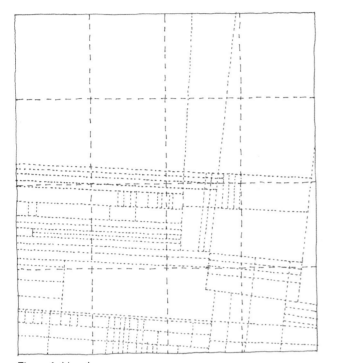

Figure 1: Map A

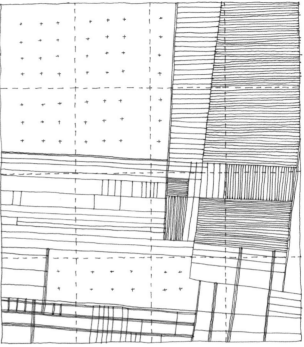

Figure 2: Map B

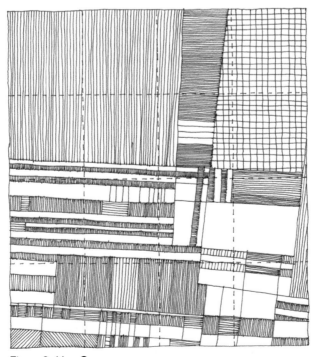

Figure 3: Map C

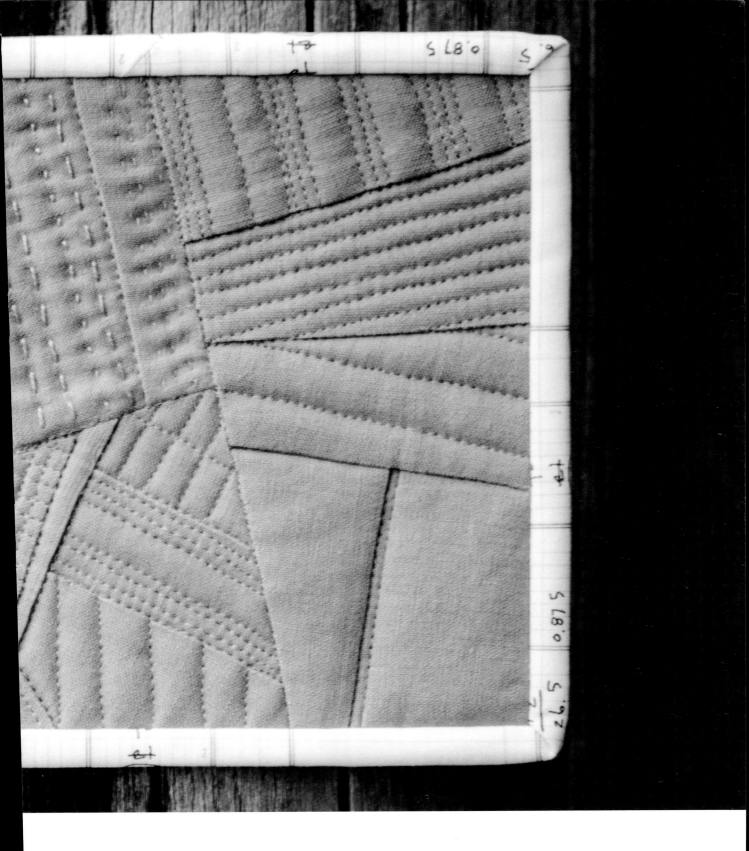

TEXTURE

YOU CAN THINK OF TEXTURE AS HAVING TWO KINDS OF IMPACT: THE VISUAL AND THE TACTILE. Visual texture is often found on the surface, and physical texture can be found in the substrate. When quilting, you can achieve both visual and physical texture by way of your thread choice, quilting design, and density.

Looking at the projects in this book, you can see how texture is at play in a variety of ways. In some quilts, it may be the surface design of the fabric that makes the most prominent statement, and in others it may be the quilting that brings the surface to life. Compare the Fringe version of Emphasis with the Flame version of Circle Lattice (see right). The quilting in Fringe creates a rough texture and plays off the surface design of the inner gray fabric, whereas the quilting in Flame is clean and orderly and complements the rhythm and character created in the piecing. Had I decided to switch the textural approach in these two projects, I could have juxtaposed roughness with rigidity in Flame and created pattern from order in Fringe.

TIP: Quilt making is the perfect medium in which to explore texture.

The tactile aspect of texture is intrinsic to quilt making, and it is no surprise that we are tempted to introduce texture so frequently in our work. At the fabric store it is almost impossible to keep your hands off the bolts of fabric. There is nothing better than that first snuggle under a new quilt, and you probably find yourself constantly running your fingers over heavily textured quilting. The following project provides you with a great opportunity to play with all kinds of texture.

Compare the texture of the quilting in Fringe, above, with the quilting in Flame.

PROJECT | I have always liked the idea of a crazy quilt, as they often incorporate many different fabric textures and interesting piecing techniques. I appreciate traditional versions for their use of decorative embroidery stitches, which do add a lot of texture, but I am more interested in taking inspiration from that style, using it in a way that works for my aesthetic and me. All that fuss is not necessary for me.

The blocks for this project were inspired by the irregular and unexpected shapes you might see in a traditional crazy quilt, but it is paper pieced. There will be no decorative stitches, nested pieces, or any of that fussiness to worry about.

Another bonus to paper piecing is that it makes it a breeze to incorporate even the trickiest, slipperiest, most unstable substrates—the paper will stabilize them! Perfect. What an appropriate project to explore texture.

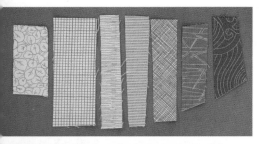

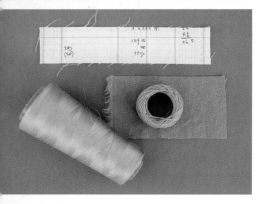

CRAZY | red

This red version is an exploration in surface texture. I incorporated small-scale prints from the red family that supplied a lot of visual texture to add interest within the smaller piecing in this project. I went with a monochromatic palette that has a wide range of contrast.

When there is so much surface texture in a project, as in this one, an overall quilting approach can work really well. Anything more detailed or varied than that could easily get lost.

CRAZY | blue

Substrate texture is at play in the blue version. I used fabrics in a wide range of substrates, from quilting cotton to drapey, soft silk to linen, corduroy, and velveteen. This is a project you will not be able to stop touching. It might not be easy to mix these fabrics together with another technique, but paper piecing is a perfect way to do it. It stabilizes the fabrics and makes them very easy to work with. This is a scenario in which I would recommend prewashing your fabrics (see page 118).

CRAZY | gray

In this final version, the plan was to highlight as much quilted texture as possible. To do that, I first decided to work in a singular fabric palette. I used Essex Linen in Steel for both its color (it's a great gray and a workable color to show dimension) and its sturdy composition that is wonderful for quilting. I also differentiated each pieced section by changing up the quilting style, direction, and density. Mixing machine stitches with hand stitches introduced an even wider range of textures.

CRAZY

Finished Block Size: 6" x 6"

Finished sizes: 6½" x 6½" coasters (set of four), 14½" x 28½" runner, 35½" x 38½" wall

Note: *Sizes are referred to in the following order: coaster (runner, wall).*

MATERIALS

Block fabrics: ⅝ yard (1 yard, 2⅞ yard) total or 7 (14, 40) 2½" strips

Border fabric (for runner and wall sizes only): ¼ yard runner, ½ yard wall

Backing fabric: ⅜ yard (¾ yard, 2½ yards)

Binding fabric: ⅜ yard (⅜ yard, ½ yard)

Batting: four 10" squares for coasters, 23" x 37" runner, 44" x 47" wall

PREPARATION

Make 1 (2, 7*) copies each of Block Templates A, B, C, and D (pages 140-143). *You only need to make a total of 25 blocks for the wall size, so pick your favorites. This project requires 4 (8, 25) blocks total.

CUTTING INSTRUCTIONS

From block fabrics, cut 2½" strips as needed for piecing.

ASSEMBLE BLOCKS

Use the 2½" strips to paper piece the blocks (page 127). On Block D #7, paper piece by cutting to fit (page 128). Refer to Figure 1 for assembly.

ASSEMBLE QUILT TOP

Coasters are ready for you to quilt. For others lay out finished blocks 4 columns across and 2 rows down for the runner, and 5 columns across and 5 rows down for the wall hanging. Sew blocks together along solid seam lines. Remove paper in seam allowance after sewing each seam. Press seams so they nest (page 119).

Refer to the Border Workshop (page 36) before attaching your borders.

Cut and attach 2½" (3" for wall) borders to sides. Press seams toward borders. Cut and attach 1½" (3" for wall) borders at the top and 1½" (6" for wall) at the bottom. Press seams toward borders.

Carefully remove and recycle all remaining paper.

QUILT FINISHING

Baste and quilt as desired. Cut binding fabric into 4 (3, 4) strips 2½" wide and see page 128 for finishing instructions.

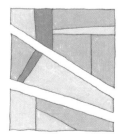
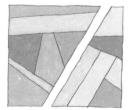

Figure 1

TECHNIQUES

PRE-WASHING YOUR FABRIC

I know that many people have strong opinions about this topic. Personally, my thoughts about pre-washing are not much different than they are for everything else I do—which is to say: it depends. In general, I like the idea of pre-washing, but I give myself permission to be flexible. There are many times when I have found a piece of fabric in my stash perfect for something I am working on, and if I am ready to go and it is not pre-washed then I am not going to think twice about using it. If you buy only quilting cottons from our wonderful independent quilt shops, you know that they are top-notch quality and are not likely to give you too much trouble (such as shrinking excessively or bleeding when washed). But there are times when I think pre-washing is a must.

I love working with a variety of substrates—quilting cotton, voile, linen, silk, corduroy, sateen, velveteen, or any other interesting options that pop up—but I'm mindful of the challenges each presents and am very careful.

The first rule is that it is important to always make sure your fabrics are of good quality. In deviating from the norm of quilting cottons, you are opening yourself up for potential surprises. Make sure that everything comes from a trustworthy source, and you'll mitigate the risks of a surprise at least a little bit.

The other thing to consider when working with multiple substrates is that they are made from different fibers using different techniques, and therefore have varying physical properties. A quilting cotton isn't composed of the same fibers as a heavy-weight linen, which is why these fabrics feel, look, and act differently. This is also why using them together can be so much fun. Because of their inherent differences, I always pre-wash anything that isn't quilting cotton; if I'm using them together, I pre-wash the quilting cotton, too. That way I eliminate some of the surprise of which-will-shrink-how-much, putting all the fabrics on the same page, so to speak. There is still some risk, but, hey, you did what you could.

BASIC PIECING

STITCH LENGTH
When basting, use 5.0mm machine stitch length. When piecing, use a 1.5mm machine stitch length. When topstitching or quilting with a walking foot, use 3.0mm machine stitch length.

SEAM ALLOWANCE
Seam allowances for machine piecing are a scant ¼" unless noted otherwise. Seam allowances for hand appliqué are ⅛" unless noted otherwise.

PRESSING
In most situations, press seams in a direction that reduces bulk. When attaching blocks together in rows, alternate the direction you are pressing the seam allowances so the seams nest (see right) when they come together.

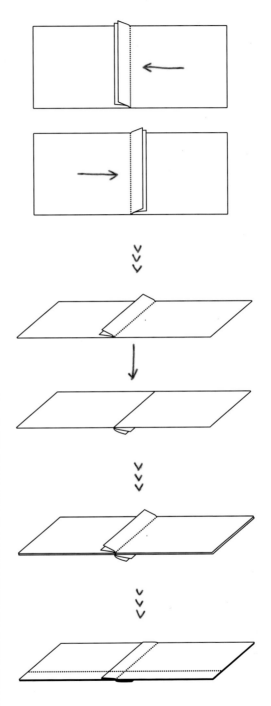

Pressing seam allowances so they nest will reduce bulk at seam intersections

NEEDLE-TURN APPLIQUÉ

SUPPLIES

Basting thread in contrasting color (such as Aurifil 50 wt. cotton) This thread is strong and thin—a winning combination for just about anything.

Appliqué thread in coordinating color (such as Aurifil 50 wt. cotton) 50 wt. is fine enough to make your stitches disappear. If you want to make more of a statement, you can use a thicker 40 wt.

Appliqué needle (such as Clover Gold Eye Sharps No. 10) A fine, flexible, sharp needle for appliqué. These handle tight corners and leave no trace.

Appliqué pins (such as Clover Appliqué No. 12) These pins are only ¾" long so they hold appliqué panels in place without causing too many pricks while handling.

Large fabric scissors (such as Karen Kay Buckley 7½" Perfect Scissors) Sharp scissors are a must for appliqué. These will cut through multiple layers with ease and precision.

Small fabric scissors (such as Karen Kay Buckley 4" Perfect Scissors) These are perfect for snipping your inner curves and points without leaving excess thread behind.

Removable marking tool (such as Pilot Frixion pen) It's always important to test any marking tools before you use them. This is what I use most often.

Seam gauge (such as Dritz sewing gauge) I find this gauge to be very handy for many situations, especially hand appliqué. The clear markings and compact shape make it easy hold and use.

Iron (such as Rowenta) For any quilting and sewing needs, an effective, hot iron is a must.

Heavy paper or template plastic (for copying template) You can always use paper or cardstock, but for something more durable, template plastic works well and can be easy to use. For larger appliqués (like Circle Lattice), you may choose to use freezer paper.

Other supplies: thimble, needle threader, thread conditioner (such as Thread Heaven) For appliqué, I protect my finger with leather ThimblePads (by Colonial Needle). Needle threaders can be useful for threading the fine-eye of an appliqué needle, and thread conditioners can be used to strengthen thread and prevent knots.

BASIC STEPS

Pin appliqué in place with appliqué pins. Using contrasting thread, hand (or machine) baste appliqué panel to background ¼" from raw edge with long basting stitches. Remove basting pins as you go.

Thread appliqué needle with matching thread and knot at one end. Fold raw edge of appliqué under to meet basting stitch, creating ⅛" turn-under allowance. Bring threaded needle up through all layers close to edge.

Baste ¼" from appliqué edge

Background fabric (right side up)

Appliqué fabric (right side up)

Pin in place

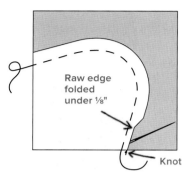

Raw edge folded under ⅛"

Knot

Continuing to fold raw edge in to meet basting stitch, direct needle down through background fabric at folded appliqué edge (perpendicular to the appliqué edge) and back up through appliqué panel ⅛" from previous stitch.

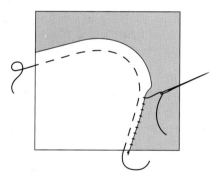

Continue around appliqué until all edges are folded under and stitched down. Knot threads at back of project.

After appliqué is fully attached, remove basting stitches. Press flat.

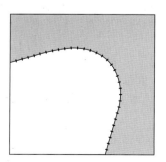

APPLIQUÉING AT CONCAVE CURVES, CORNERS, AND POINTS

At concave curves, clip into seam allowance ⅟₁₆" along curve. The tighter the curve, the more clips you will need. Space evenly for a more fluid curve.

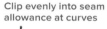

Clip evenly into seam allowance at curves

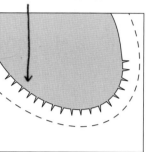

At corners, fold each side under as you come to it to create a defined corner. Use extra stitches at corner to secure.

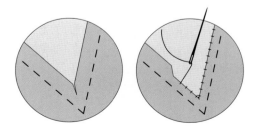

At interior points, clip fabric ⅟₁₆" at point and fold both raw edges under using needle to work edges in. Use extra stitches at point to secure.

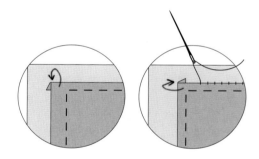

PAPER PIECING

SUPPLIES
Thread in coordinating color
(such as Aurifil Cotton 50 wt.)

Sewing machine needles

Open-toe foot (see note, below.)

Rotary cutter

Cutting mat

Rulers (see note, below.)

Iron

Paper for copying template
(see note, below.)

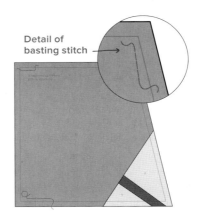

Detail of basting stitch

PREPARATION, SUPPLIES, AND GENERAL TIPS

My favorite paper for paper piecing is recycled 20 lb. weight office paper. The recycled paper is a bit thinner than regular, plus it's a more responsible choice. The weight of this paper gives the block excellent body when working with all types of fabric.

Tip: It is always desirable to have your ironing and cutting stations next to your sewing area. I set up my own workspace so that I can swivel my chair between each station.

Before starting a block, write notes about fabric placement on the paper template as a reference.

Holding the template up to the light will help you locate and align fabric and/or marked lines.

Using large basting stitches (5.0mm) works especially well for holding large and/or awkward pieces of fabric in place when paper piecing the blocks. Pins can also be used as an alternative.

Paper piecing is worked on the *wrong* side of the printed paper template. Take note of this relationship in the directions and corresponding diagrams. You will be sewing with the printed side of the paper facing *up*. Your fabric will be underneath the paper, against the sewing machine.

When paper piecing, shorten your machine stitch length to 1.5mm. Using a shorter stitch makes for a tighter seam. It also perforates the paper more, making removal much easier.

Use an open-toe foot or any foot that allows good visibility of the sewing area.

Work in numerical order, always starting with areas labeled 1 and 2 on the block template and continuing with 3, 4, etc., until the entire block is pieced.

You can use specialty quarter- and eighth-inch rulers when paper piecing, but I tend to favor a regular ruler with easy-to-read quarter-inch markings.

Remove the paper in the seam allowance after sewing two blocks together. This makes paper removal much easier in the end.

PAPER PIECING BY SIZE

Use this technique for Emphasis (page 90). Refer to instructions for suggested cut fabric size. Start at areas marked 1 and 2. Place fabric 1 (RIGHT side *up*) over area 1 on paper template (INK side *down*) with long edge extending ¼" into area 2. Position fabric 2 over area 2, aligning with long side of 1 and making sure it is covering sides at area 2 evenly.

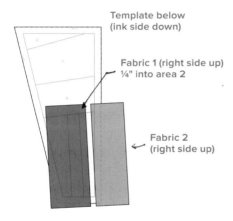

Template below
(ink side down)

Fabric 1 (right side up)
¼" into area 2

Fabric 2
(right side up)

Flip fabric 2 onto fabric 1 so that RIGHT sides are *together* and both extend ¼" into area 2.

¼" into area 2 (RIGHT sides *together*)

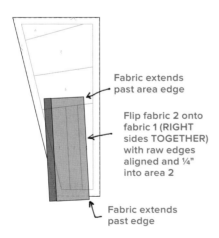

Fabric extends
past area edge

Flip fabric 2 onto
fabric 1 (RIGHT
sides TOGETHER)
with raw edges
aligned and ¼"
into area 2

Fabric extends
past edge

Hold (and/or pin or use long basting stitches) both fabric pieces together and flip over entire stack (including paper). Stitch along marked line between areas 1 and 2, backstitching at beginning and end of seam; sew the full length of the line.

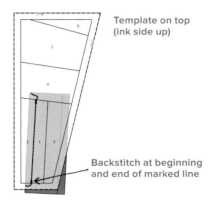

Template on top
(ink side up)

Backstitch at beginning
and end of marked line

Trim threads. Flip over. Remove any basting stitches. Press fabric 2 open. Flip the paper with the ink side facing *up*. Fold paper template back along next seam line between areas 1 and 3. Trim fabric ¼" from fold/seam line. Flip over and unfold paper. Center fabric 3 over area 3.

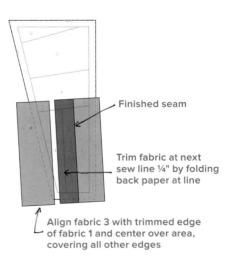

Finished seam

Trim fabric at next
sew line ¼" by folding
back paper at line

Align fabric 3 with trimmed edge
of fabric 1 and center over area,
covering all other edges

Flip fabric 3 over (RIGHT sides *together*) along trimmed edge. Hold (and/or baste) together and flip over stack. Stitch along marked line between areas 2 and 3, backstitching at beginning and end. Flip over. Trim threads. Remove any basting stitches. Press fabric 3 open. Repeat these steps covering each section in numerical order until block is complete, making sure fabric extends generously past template edge. Once block template is covered, use ruler to trim excess fabric ¼" from outer sewing lines on block template. Leave paper attached.

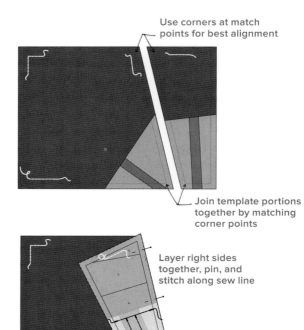

Use corners at match points for best alignment

Join template portions together by matching corner points

Layer right sides together, pin, and stitch along sew line

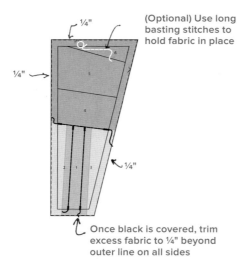

(Optional) Use long basting stitches to hold fabric in place

¼"

¼"

¼"

Once black is covered, trim excess fabric to ¼" beyond outer line on all sides

Remove paper in seam allowance, and press seam to one side.

Set first portion of finished block aside. Make remainder of block.

To attach template parts, flip RIGHT sides *together*, matching corner points and aligning raw edges. Sew along seam line.

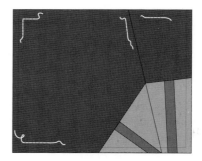

Make next blocks and repeat until all blocks are completed.

PAPER PIECING BY STRIP

Use this technique for Facing East (page 67) and Crazy (page 115). Cut strips according to project instructions.

Position fabric 1 strip (RIGHT side *up*) over area 1 (template INK side *down*) with long, raw edge aligned with first seam line and extending over seamline ¼". Position fabric 2 strip (RIGHT side *up*) over area 2 aligning long, raw edge with fabric 1 strip. Trim both strips so that you have ½" excess at either end.

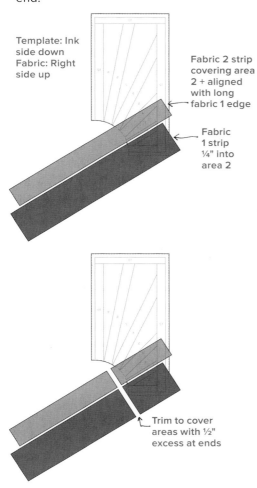

Template: Ink side down
Fabric: Right side up

Fabric 2 strip covering area 2 + aligned with long fabric 1 edge

Fabric 1 strip ¼" into area 2

Trim to cover areas with ½" excess at ends

Flip fabric 2 (RIGHT sides *together*) onto fabric 1 along trimmed edge.

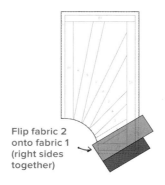

Flip fabric 2 onto fabric 1 (right sides together)

Hold (and/or baste) together and flip over. Stitch along marked seam line. Backstitch at beginning and end. Flip over. Trim threads. Press open. Trim. Fold paper template back along seam line between areas 2 and 3. Trim fabric ¼" from fold/seam line. Flip over and unfold paper. Position next strip over area 3. Trim to cover area with ½" excess at either end.

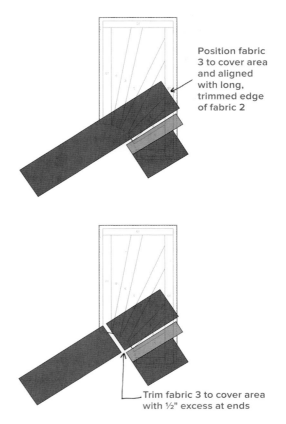

Position fabric 3 to cover area and aligned with long, trimmed edge of fabric 2

Trim fabric 3 to cover area with ½" excess at ends

Flip fabric 3 onto fabric 2 along trimmed edge. Hold (and/or baste) together and flip over. Stitch along marked line. Backstitch at beginning and end. Flip over. Trim threads. Press open. Repeat until block is covered.

PAPER PIECING BY CUTTING TO FIT

Use this technique for Crazy (page 115) on block D, area 7. Position 2½" strip lengthwise (RIGHT side *up*) to cover area 7 with excess fabric at all sides. Use long basting stitches or pins to hold fabric in place and flip over. Fold paper template back at first seamline to trim excess fabric ¼" from seamline. Flip over. Position next strip for area 8, and continue.

REMOVING THE PAPER

I keep the paper on my blocks as long as I can. Paper keeps the blocks clean and free of extra thread, lint, and dust, and it also keeps the blocks from distorting. However, paper can also get too bulky and uncomfortable to work with, especially when working on larger projects. In those cases, I recommend keeping the paper on until all sides of the block have been sewn into place. At that point you can carefully remove the paper and recycle it.

QUILT BLOCKING

Blocking your quilt basically means getting it wet so that you can lay it flat so that it dries and sets up in its final state. I end up blocking many of my quilts because it is a good way to remove any distortion that may have occurred during quilting. I often quilt my quilts very heavily, and blocking is a way to soften and balance out some of that.

HOW TO BLOCK

The way that I block my quilts is pretty simple. Before adding any binding or trimming off my excess batting and backing, I throw the quilt in the washing machine on delicate or the hand-wash cycle, using cold water and at least one Color Catcher™. When the cycle ends, smooth the quilt on a floor or bed large enough for it to lie flat. Smooth and flatten by eye, or use rulers and other guides to make sure the borders are straight and flat. Then turn on a fan and let the quilt dry fully.

Once the quilt is dry and you are happy with its final shape, trim the excess batting and backing and bind as usual.

QUILT FINISHING

Cut backing and batting to size.

Baste together quilt sandwich with backing on bottom (RIGHT side *out*), batting in center, and pieced panel on top (RIGHT side *out*).

Quilt as desired. See Quilting Workshop (page 99) for tips.

Trim layer edges evenly. Cut 2½" x width-of-fabric strips for binding. See project instructions for strip numbers. (Optional: Use scraps from blocks to create a scrappy binding look.) Sew ends together diagonally and press seams open. Fold binding strip in half wrong sides together and use your favorite binding technique or see the Quilt Making Basics on the Lucky Spool Website (www.luckyspool.com).

STUDIO WORKBOOK

Your turn! A blank page (or a blank project outline) is the perfect place to start illustrating your project in your own way. Let yourself plan colors, fabrics, and quilting strategies on these blank templates that are a reflection of you. Have at it.

SCALES

BULLS EYE

Wall

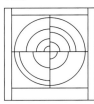

Baby

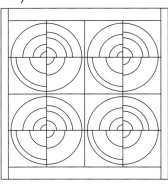

Throw

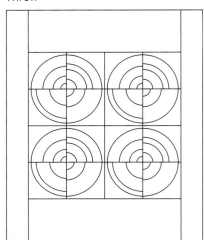

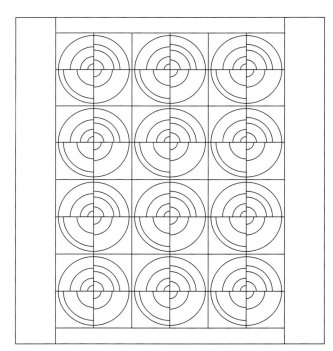

Full/Queen

CIRCLE LATTICE

Wall

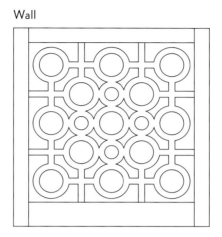

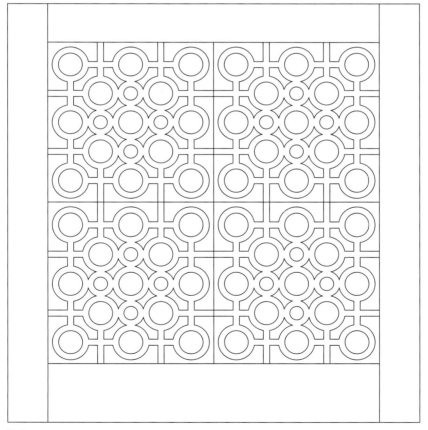

Full

FACING EAST

Throw

Wall/Baby

Runner

Full/Queen

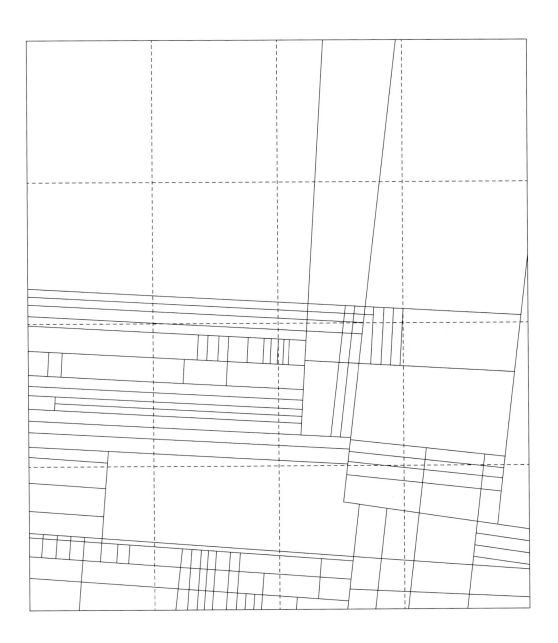

EMPHASIS: STRIPE/MEDALLION

Wall/Baby

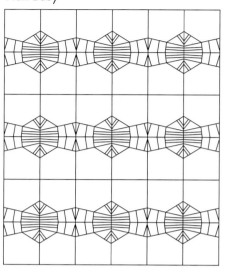

Runner

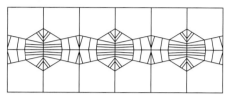

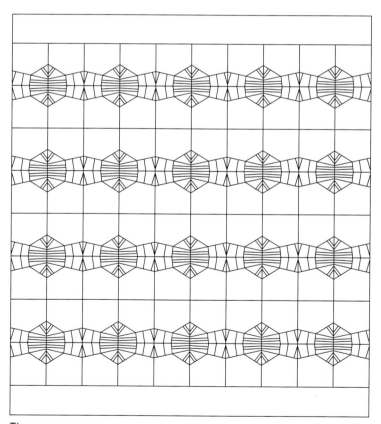

Throw

EMPHASIS: FRINGE

Runner

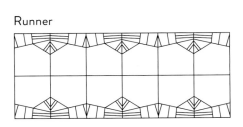

Wall/Baby

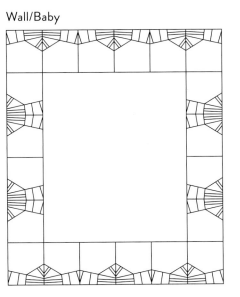

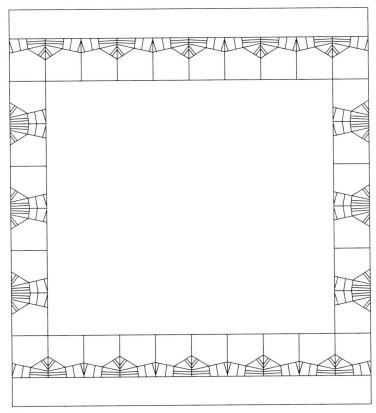

Throw

AERIAL GROVE

Runner

4" x 10½"

3" x 26"

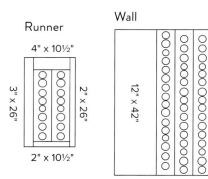

2" x 26"

2" x 10½"

Wall

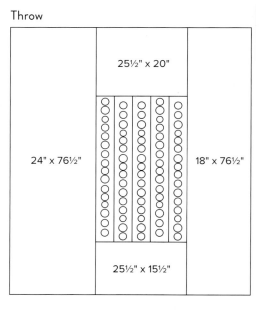

12" x 42"

6" x 42"

Throw

25½" x 20"

24" x 76½"

18" x 76½"

25½" x 15½"

25½" x 20"

37" x 80½"

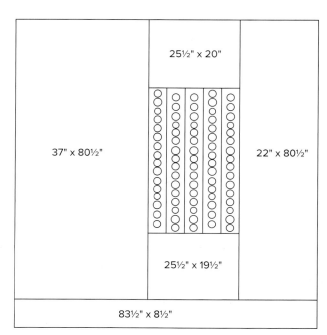

22" x 80½"

25½" x 19½"

83½" x 8½"

Full/Queen

CRAZY

Coasters

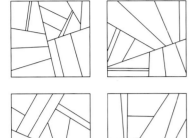

Runner

Wall

TEMPLATES

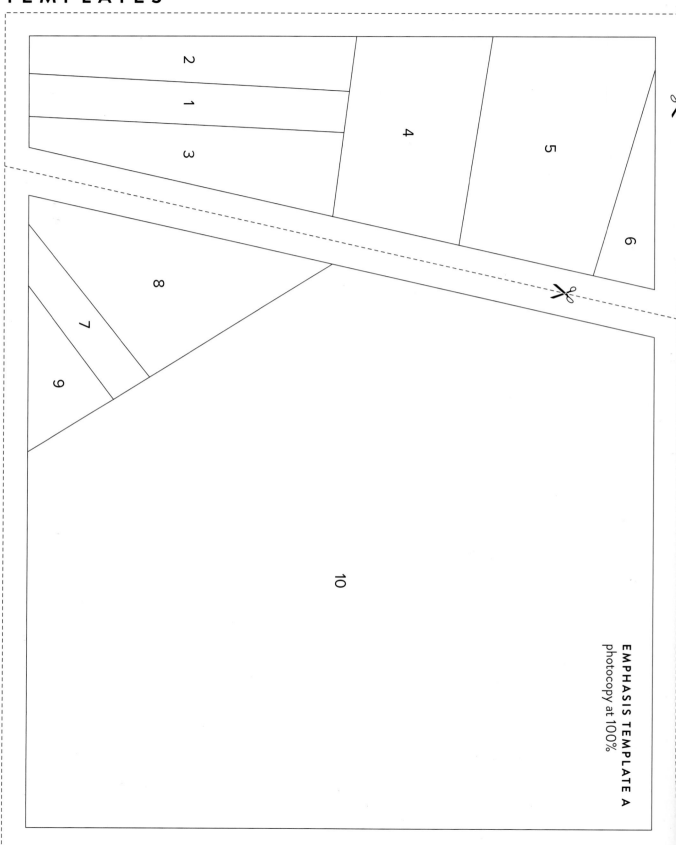

EMPHASIS TEMPLATE A
photocopy at 100%

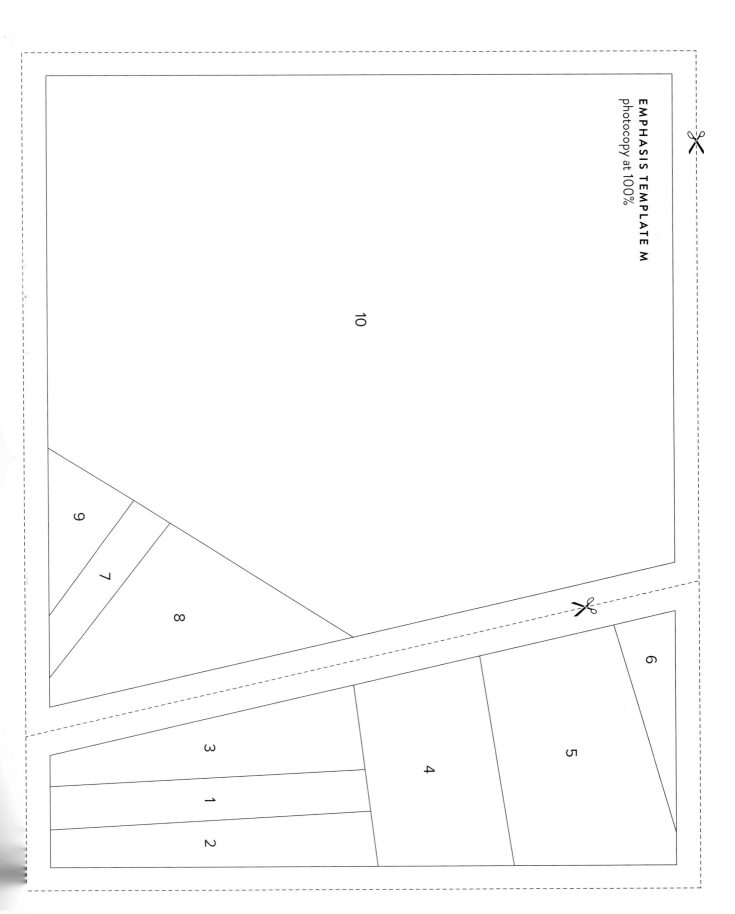

EMPHASIS TEMPLATE M
photocopy at 100%

CRAZY TEMPLATE A
photocopy at 100%

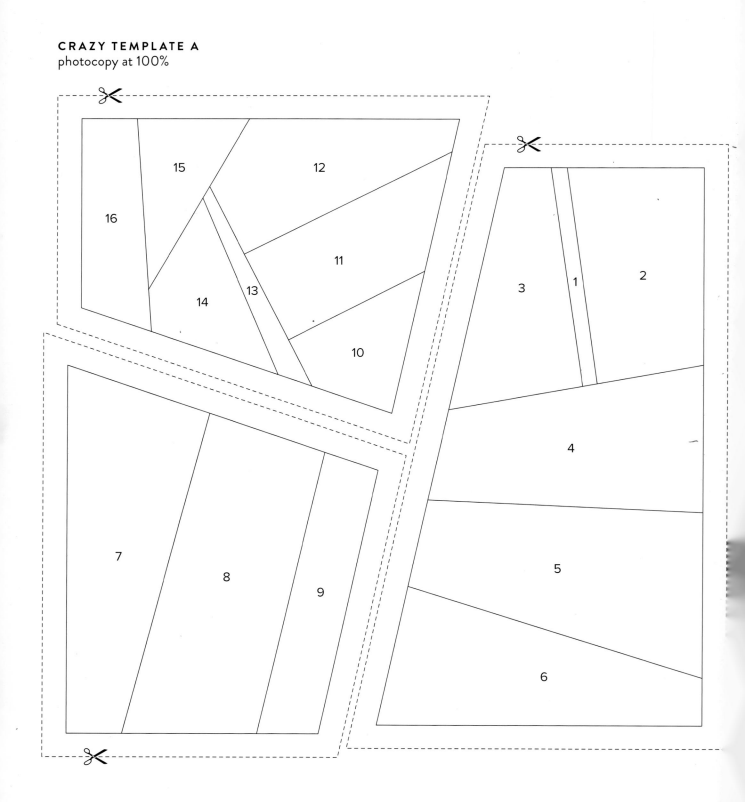

CRAZY TEMPLATE B
photocopy at 100%

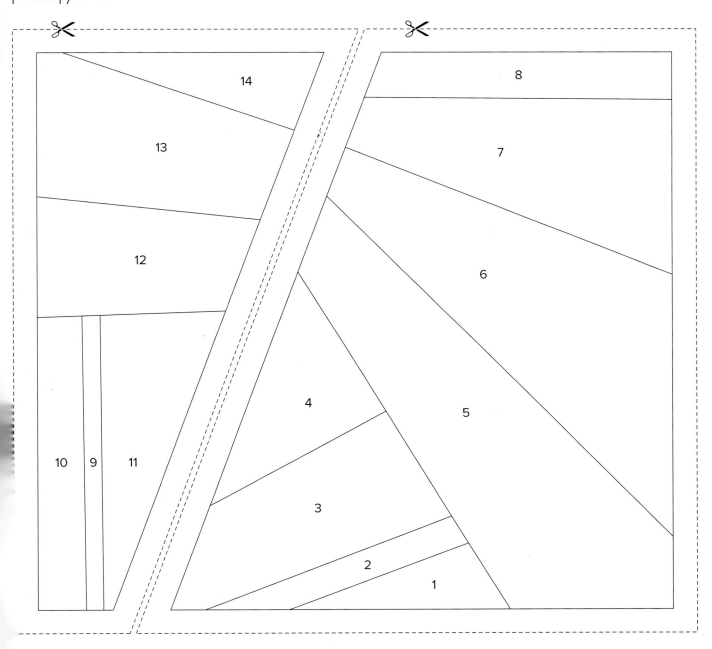

CRAZY TEMPLATE C
photocopy at 100%

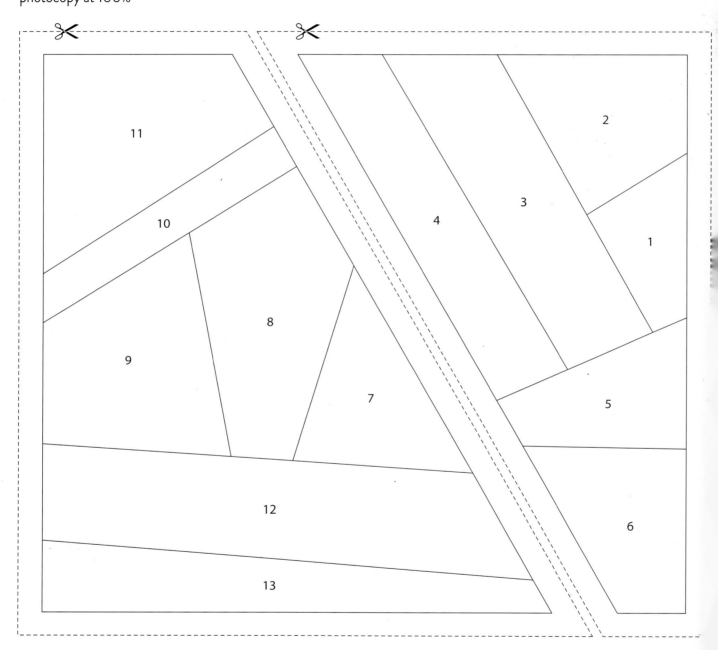

CRAZY TEMPLATE D
photocopy at 100%

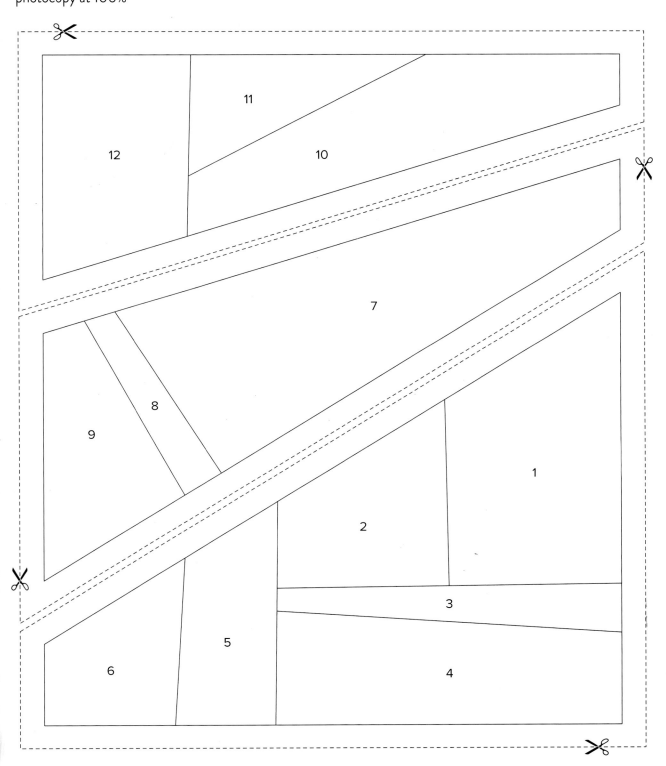

RESOURCES

Here are some of my favorite sewing supplies and places you can find them.

AURIFIL
www.aurifil.com
- Thread 50 wt. (For machine and hand piecing, machine quilting)

CLOVER
www.clover-usa.com
- Appliqué needles (Clover Gold Eye Sharps No. 10)
- Appliqué pins (Clover Appliqué No. 12)
- Clover Wonder Clips (great for binding)
- Protect and Grip thimble (for hand quilting)
- Glasshead pins (for piecing and general sewing)

COLONIAL NEEDLE
www.colonialneedle.com
- Big stitch (quilting) needles
- ThimblePad (for hand appliqué)

DEAR STELLA
www.dearstelladesign.com
- Fabric

DRITZ
www.dritz.com
- Seam gauge

JANOME
www.janome.com
- Sewing machines

KAREN KAY BUCKLEY
www.karenkaybuckley.com
- Scissors (7½" Perfect Scissors are great for cutting out appliqué projects, especially multiple layers at a time; (4" Perfect Scissors are great for clipping seams when appliquéing.)

OLFA
www.olfa.com
- Cutting mat and rotary cutter

OMNIGRID®
www.dritz.com/brands/omnigrid/
- Rulers

PAPER SOURCE
www.paper-source.com
- Stationery supplies

PINK CASTLE FABRICS
www.pinkcastlefabrics.com
- Fabric

PINK CHALK FABRICS
www.pinkchalkfabrics.com
- Fabric
- Frixion Heat Erase pens

PRESENCIA
www.presenciaamerica.com
- Perle cotton thread for big stitch quilting (I use No. 8 and No. 12)

ROBERT KAUFMAN
www.robertkaufman.com
- Fabric
- Kona cotton, Essex linen, and all other substrates

ROWENTA
www.rowentausa.com
- Iron

SHOUT® COLOR CATCHER®
www.shoutitout.com/en-US/Products/Pages/shout-color-catcher.aspx

SIMPLICITY
www.simplicity.com
- EZ template plastic

SOAK WASH INC
www.soakwash.com
- Flatter (starch-free ironing spray)

SUPERBUZZY
www.superbuzzy.com
- Fabric

THREAD HEAVEN
www.threadheaven.com
- Thread Conditioner